Praise for *Shipwrecks of Lake Ontario*

Kennard's *Shipwrecks of Lake Ontario: My Journey of Discovery* summarizes many years of productive research and field work by the author and his teammates, and it very successfully documents the unique discoveries and the observations that they have achieved, including several of the Great Lakes earliest shipwrecks.
      Pat Labadie, Grandfather of Great Lakes Archaeology

Jim Kennard and his contributing authors, photographers and illustrators have created a highly readable account of some of Lake Ontario's most fascinating shipwrecks. The tales of discovery are lively and engaging. Jim's journey from treasure hunter to historian and preservation advocate lends authenticity to his already compelling stories. Reading this book, a glimpse into the rich history and traditions of Lake Ontario's navigation emerges. The well-chosen illustrations and photographs document the astonishing level of preservation the lake's deep and cold water affords its shipwrecks. With knowledge comes responsibility. We must act to protect these and other extraordinary wreck sites and underwater graves from unwarranted intrusions, damage and indifference.
      Mark Peckham, Trustee, Hudson River Maritime Museum
      Retired, New York State Division for Historic Preservation

Shipwrecks of Lake Ontario not only provides an amazing, first-hand view of the Lake's many sunken time capsules, but also tells the fascinating stories of how the wrecks were researched, located and identified. Author Jim Kennard is a pioneer in the field of remote sensing and a consummate seeker of lost things. This book tells the story of his long career probing the depths as well as his many fantastic historical discoveries. Shipwrecks of Lake Ontario includes compelling discovery stories of some of the earliest and most historic ships ever found on the Great Lakes including the HMS Ontario (1780), which lies almost completely intact in the extreme depths of the Lake, as well as the sloop Washington (1797) and many other early and important Great Lakes vessels. This is a must-have book for anyone interested in the shipwrecks of Lake Ontario or in the early history of ships and shipping on the Great Lakes.
      Brendon Baillod, Great Lakes Historian

Explorer Club Fellow, Jim Kennard, documents in a fascinating book his discovery of important historical ships that shipwrecked or disappeared during Lake Ontario's raging storms. Complete with sharp pictures and images, impeccable research, and well-documented facts, it starts with his discovery of the British warship *Ontario* (the oldest found in the Great Lakes) that dated back to the Revolutionary War and naval history. A total of 35 wrecks are so detailed, including the sloop *Washington* (the 2nd so oldest). These are described in similar standout fashion that highlight Kennard's illustrious career.

> Dennis Powers, author of *Treasure Ship*, *Sentinel of the Seas*,
> *Taking the Sea*, *Tales of the Seven Seas*,
> and other maritime books.

Some of the oldest, deepest and yet best preserved wrecks on the Great Lakes have been revealed thanks to the explorations of Jim Kennard and his team. And each revelation helps us better understand the story of the Great Lakes.

> Walter Lewis, Great Lakes Historian

Shipwrecks of Lake Ontario:

A Journey of Discovery

"persevere"
Jim Kennard

By Jim Kennard

Roland Stevens and Roger Pawlowski

Published by the Great Lakes Historical Society —
National Museum of the Great Lakes
Toledo, Ohio

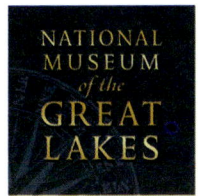

Copyright 2019 by Jim Kennard
Printed in the United States

ISBN – 978-0-940741-02-7

Editor — Christopher H. Gillcrist
Assistant Editor — Carrie E. Sowden
Graphic Design — Ellen P. Kennedy
Editorial Support — Nancy Schneider
Cover design by Jamie Kennard, Krate
Book layout by Professional Book Compositors
Printing by Baker & Taylor

Contents

Acknowledgements	*ix*
Introduction	*xi*
My Journey to Discovery	*xiii*
Where Shipwrecks are Located in Lake Ontario	*xxiii*

THE EARLY YEARS: 1980–2007

My First Discovery on Lake Ontario: The Steamer *Ellsworth*	2
St Peter, by Bob Bristol	5
Last Voyage of the Steamer *Homer Warren*	11
Lake Ontario Claims the Schooner *Etta Belle* in Calm Weather	17
Salt Ship	22
The Final Chapter of USCG Cable Boat *CG-56022*	27
60-Fathom Shipwreck: The Schooner *William Elgin*	36
The Artist and the *Orcadian*	40
Fatal Fire on the Steamer *Samuel F. Hodge*	45
The Wreck of the *W. Y. Emery*, by John Albright	49

THE *ONTARIO*: 2008

The British Warship *Ontario*	54
Weather Behind the Sinking of HMS *Ontario*, by Robert Hamilton	63
Ontario, A Model Built at 1:48 Scale, by Ray Peacock	72

LATER YEARS: 2008–2018

Unexpected Rare Shipwreck Discovery: A Daggerboard Schooner	86
A Lucky Wind Makes for Discovery of the Schooner *C. Reeve*	91
Queen of the Lakes	95
Tragedy in a November Gale	101
Schooner *Atlas*: She Sank Like a Stone	105
Ocean Wave: The Schooner That Would not Sink	109
Canadian Steamer *Roberval*	114
Above and Below Lake Ontario: USAF C-45	121
Another Daggerboard: *Three Brothers*	127
Steamship *Nisbet Grammer*: Lake Ontario's Largest Shipwreck	131

Canal Boats From 1800s Discovered in Lake Ontario	*136*
Early Propeller Steamship *Bay State*	*139*
Canadian Schooner *Royal Albert* "Derailed" in Lake Ontario	*144*
Discovery of a Great Lakes Treasure: Sloop *Washington*	*148*
Remains of the Schooner *Hartford* Found	*154*
Rare Sailing Craft Found in Lake Ontario	*160*

Appendices

Ford Shoals: A Most Dangerous Place	*166*
Mexico Bay: Graveyard of Ships	*169*
Sunken Houseboats off Oswego	*173*
Recreational Diving on Shipwrecks near Oswego	*175*
Authors' Biographies	*180*

To Marilyn

Thank you for your love, encouragement, and support that made my journey of exploration and discovery possible.

Acknowledgements

I never thought about writing a book when I began searching for shipwrecks in Lake Ontario. It was only after years of news media releases and communications with Mark Peckham of the New York State Office of Parks, Recreation and Historic Preservation that I began to seriously consider telling the story of my adventures. Many thanks go to Mark for suggesting that I compile my research with our exploration team's underwater images, sketches, and paintings. In 2011 our team was very pleased when the National Museum of the Great Lakes became our sponsor. In 2014 during a meeting with Chris Gillcrist, Executive Director, he mentioned the possibility of the museum publishing a book of our shipwreck discoveries. I knew that writing it would be a big undertaking but I had no idea how big! Shipwreck searching, hiking the Adirondack and Catskill Mountains, and family obligations left me little time to devote to writing a book. That changed when I had ankle surgery in January 2017 that laid me up for several months. If I was going to have to sit in a chair with my foot up in the air I figured I better write that book while there were few distractions. Towards the end of the year I had four chapters remaining and they were the hardest to compose since I was now mobile again and taking time to sit down and write was difficult for me. Now that it's done I hope you, the reader, will enjoy my journey of discovery.

There are a number of people involved in the development of this book who have worked diligently to make it a successful read. Starting with my wife, Marilyn, an excellent editor, who reviewed the stories, returning them to me multiple times for additions, clarifications and rewrites. Marilyn, thank you so much for all your time and patience. Funding for the publishing effort of *Shipwrecks of Lake Ontario: A Journey of Discovery* comes in part from a grant from the Shumway Foundation which has been a wonderful supporter of The National Museum of the Great Lakes. Chris Gillcrist did a fantastic job of editing and reviewing the book with me in 2018. At the same time Carrie Sowden, Archaeological Director, edited and fact checked each chapter. Thank you also to Ellen Kennedy, Educational Manager, for reviewing and providing editorial assistance. Final editing was done by Nancy Schneider, Editor of *Inland Seas*, the quarterly journal of the National Museum of the Great Lakes. To the many people I've met along the way, fellow explorers, and nautical history enthusiasts who have lightened the load and brightened my days, I will always be grateful for your company, insight and encouragement. Thank you.

Introduction

Searching for shipwrecks in the Great Lakes began in the 1800s when there was a cargo or vessel worth salvaging. The search methods were crude and might entail dragging a line with a large grappling hook or using two ships with a long weighted line between them to find the missing target. The introduction of the electronic depth finder made it much easier to locate a shipwreck but it was still very time consuming since you had to pass right over the wreck in order to see a protrusion on the bottom. When side scan sonar systems became available, you no longer had to run right over the top of a shipwreck. The high resolution sonar created an image similar to an aerial photograph of the sea floor. A search could cover a large swath of up to 2000 feet in one pass depending if the search object was large enough. In the 1970s there were only a few side scan units being used on the Great Lakes. Several were owned by commercial marine companies and a few by shipwreck hunters seeking treasure. These units cost tens of thousands of dollars. By the 1980s a few more side scan sonar units were deployed on the lakes but still just a handful. Today, side scan sonar units are much more common but still are extremely expensive costing $20,000 or more for the very good ones.

The high cost of searching for shipwrecks is not limited to side scanning sonar equipment. Fuel, boat maintenance, towing equipment, and time make this hobby quite expensive. State and provincial regulations have long prevented shipwreck hunters from financially benefiting from their discoveries as recovery of artifacts from these wrecks has been outlawed for decades. Today, it's not monetary rewards that these shipwreck enthusiasts seek. The treasure is in the maritime history that we all hope to discover. Today, it is unlikely to be the first person to climb a particular mountain but it's still possible to be the first to discover a sunken ship. Fortunately, there are still many shipwrecks in the Great Lakes just waiting to be discovered.

Within the pages of this book are the tales of some of the historic shipwrecks that have been lost and found off the southern shore of Lake Ontario in New York State. Follow along on the journeys of discovery undertaken by modern day explorers as they try to locate these ships and reveal their secrets. Enjoy!

My Journey of Discovery

During the course of writing this book I pondered the question, "Where did this fascination with exploration and the discovery of shipwrecks begin?" For me exploring started early. As far back as I can remember, I explored the woods near where I grew up in Peekskill, New York, and as I grew older, I roamed farther and farther away from home. When I was seven I joined the Cub Scouts and three years later the Boy Scouts. The Scouts gave me the chance to learn many outdoor skills and to experience overnight camping trips in northern Westchester County and in the deep woods of the Adirondack Mountains. I eventually became an Eagle Scout, the highest rank in the Boy Scouts.

My interest in shipwrecks and SCUBA (self-contained underwater breathing apparatus) diving, well, that all started with Ralph Sylvester. In 1970 I lost my first job as an electrical engineer when my employer, General Dynamics (GD), moved out of Rochester, New York. The recession in those years left many GD employees out of work for a long time. I was extremely fortunate to get a job almost immediately at the Rochester Products Division of General Motors. Back then, there were about 50 people in the department all located in one big room with desks lined up in rows with no individual cubicles. We worked the same hours as those in the union. Five minutes before the end of the workday, everyone would be at their desk straightening their pencils and papers ready for the clock to signal quitting time. It was during this time that I was able to chat with my "desk neighbor," Ralph Sylvester. He started SCUBA diving in the 1960s and would talk about his adventures on shipwrecks in the Great Lakes. One in particular was the steamer *Charles Price* that turned turtle and sank in Lake Huron during the great storm of 1913. I was fascinated with Ralph's stories — and this sport sounded intriguing. SCUBA diving in the early 1970s was rising in popularity and the local YMCA offered classes several times a year. I signed up immediately and after several months of lectures and training in the pool, I was ready to take the two required open-water dives for certification. Over the next two years I spent my time scratching around on the bottom of Canandaigua Lake, one of the New York Finger Lakes, about 10 miles south of where I lived. One day a friend invited me to dive on a wreck in the St. Lawrence River at Alexandria Bay, New York. The wooden steamer *Islander* had burned at the dock in 1909 and could be reached easily since it was just down a steep river bank at a depth of 40 feet. There wasn't much left of the *Islander*, but it was exciting to finally dive on a shipwreck. My dive partner, curious if there was anything of interest left on this burnt out hulk, sifted through the ashes with his hand and lo and behold found a medallion with the image of an Indian on its face. Fabulous! This was a piece of historical treasure! I was now hooked on diving on shipwrecks.

Around that time, the wreck of the three-masted schooner *St Peter* was found off Pultneyville, New York, about 30 miles east of Rochester. The wreck was buoyed and located in 110 feet of water, which meant recreational divers like me could see it. Early in the diving season one weekday afternoon, I left work early with another GM diver friend to check out this schooner. Back then almost everyone was diving with wet suits since dry suits were too expensive. To counteract the cold, we would bring a jug of hot water and pour it into our wetsuits to stay warm during the dive, at least for a short while. At the depth of the *St Peter*, the year round water temperature doesn't get much above 39 degrees. My buddy and I located the buoy, secured the boat, and made the dive. Seeing a shipwreck that had not been destroyed by fire was a real treat. We arrived on the bottom at the bow and headed to the stern of the ship. We toured the entire ship moving very slowly due to the limited visibility. It was easy to run into the end of a mast or part of the general wreckage because we couldn't see much more than four or five feet. By the time I reached the cabin at the stern of the schooner, the water in my wetsuit was cold and I was shivering. It was time to ascend, but what a great adventure!

In 1972, I purchased a 24-foot pontoon boat to get to dive locations on Canandaigua Lake that couldn't be reached from shore. The next season I moved the boat to a marina at the northern end of the lake. One day I received a call that the boat was on its side. Apparently someone had hit one of the pontoons the previous night and it had filled with water causing the boat to tip over. My own boat became my first underwater salvage job! I fixed the pontoon, sold the boat, and purchased an 18-foot bowrider. For the next 35 years I used that boat for shipwreck searching in Lakes Ontario, Erie, Champlain, the New York Finger Lakes, and the Richelieu River.

Diving on a shipwreck that others had found was interesting but I wanted to find ships that no diver had been on before. Today divers are taught to leave ship artifacts alone. Years ago and before laws regarding removal of artifacts from a shipwreck were enacted by states and Canadian provinces, divers would strip ships clean of anything they could find and carry. I wanted to locate undiscovered, virgin shipwrecks. I reached out to a fellow I had worked with at General Dynamics who, in his previous job, had been involved in looking for test torpedoes underwater with a special instrument called side-scan sonar. The sonar sent out a signal that would reflect back to create an image of the underwater terrain similar to that of an aerial photograph. In the early 70s, there were only a couple of companies making side-scan sonars. They were primarily employed by geophysical survey companies to scan the bottom of the ocean to determine the best route for oil companies to lay a pipeline without running into obstructions. I thought I'd buy one until I learned what they cost. Over the next two years, I figured out how to build a side-scan sonar and looked for the pieces I would need to put a system together.

First I located a surplus mechanical recorder for sale that could be used for the recording device. I took the back seat out of my car, drove to Michigan, and loaded over 1,000 pounds of an old Navy sonar recorder with drawers of tube circuits into the back seat of my car. I stripped down the Navy recorder to several hundred pounds and built the solid state electronic circuitry necessary to run the machine. To save development time, I found a startup sonar company, Klein Associates, which agreed to sell me a used sonar sensor called a towfish. With the help of my wife, I twisted my own multi-conductor tow cable by draping multiple cables between two maple trees on my front lawn. Now I had the tow cable, sonar sensor, and the guts of the recorder. The initial weight of my home-built side-scan sonar system was nearly 300 pounds, including the large car batteries to

Jim Kennard operating his home built side-scan sonar.   Image courtesy of Jim Kennard

run it. The weight of the system caused my small boat to have a permanent list to port while conducting search runs!

When I was growing up, people like Jacques Cousteau popularized underwater exploration. Others like Kip Wagner and Mel Fisher were looking for and finding sunken galleons. I wanted to do that too, but reality hits home when you consider that you have a house mortgage, car payment, new job, and the wife is talking kids! I couldn't run off and look for treasure in the Caribbean. I had responsibilities!

One day I was visiting the Rochester library looking for books on shipwrecks when I found the *Directory of Shipwrecks of the Great Lakes* by Karl Heden. Each chapter in the book was devoted to one of the Great Lakes. Even back then the author must have realized that these ships contained mostly commodities such as wheat, coal, lumber, salt, etc. I think the author, or his editor, decided to embellish the monetary value of the cargoes of these ships. One ship that stood out as having a treasure of gold and silver onboard was the "sloop *Ontario* with a payroll of $500,000 of gold and silver." It was reported to have sunk in Lake Ontario in 1780. Wonderful! I didn't need to go south to find treasure. It was right out there in the lake, practically my backyard. Once my side-scan sonar was tested and working correctly we were ready to search for the shipwreck *Ontario*. I had obtained the admiralty drawing of the *Ontario* and some information about the shipwreck disaster written by the British shortly after the ship was lost. Two of my General Motors friends, Ralph Sylvester and Paul Grabowski, and I headed west of Rochester in search of this Great Lakes treasure ship.

After a number of ventures out on the lake, I concluded that the *Ontario* was probably much farther offshore than our search area. Even if we did find the ship, we wouldn't be able to dive her as the depths in that area are well beyond the safe limits for recreational divers. After two years we gave up our search effort. The admiralty drawing would remain on my office wall for many years as a reminder of the lost "treasure" ship, *Ontario*.

In the early 70s, without the use of an accurate positioning system such as GPS (global positioning system) or LORAN-C (long-range navigation), it was nearly impossible to search for shipwrecks much more than half a mile from shore. If you had a boat equipped with a RADAR (radio detection and ranging) unit, you could search beyond this distance with difficulty. My boat was too small to be equipped with a RADAR, so I came up with a crude idea of placing several buoys a half mile apart at an approximate equal distance from shore. I would then search along a line between them using my side-scan sonar. After the initial pass, I would then move the buoys farther out into the lake and repeat the process. It was definitely a

My Journey of Discovery

very inefficient way of searching but it was the best I could do at that time. I made the buoys using a milk jug filled with Styrofoam. I then ran a long stiff wire though each jug and placed a flag on one end and a weight on the other. A thin nylon line was attached to the weighted end of the buoy utilizing a brick as the anchor. One afternoon my wife, Marilyn, accompanied me on a shipwreck search in Lake Ontario. I had set up the milk jug buoys and had just completed a run when, without much warning, a severe thunderstorm arose. Just a few minutes before, the lake had been calm. As the storm approached us the waves rapidly increased to over 3 feet. I was intent in retrieving my buoys but my wife, fearing for her life, yelled between thunder claps *"forget them!!!"* Instantly, a heavy downpour of rain hit and we quickly headed back to the launch ramp. As we were nearing shore and right next to a rocky cliff area, the motor stopped. The boat was now being blown closer and closer to the rocks as the rain poured down. I quickly realized that one of my dual gas tanks had run out of gas and I flipped the gas line switch to the other tank. Thankfully, after a couple of tries, the engine started and we narrowly avoided disaster. We made it to the launch ramp, thoroughly drenched but safe. I don't recall that Marilyn ever came out again for a shipwreck search after that lake adventure!!

Marilyn Kennard and son Douglas.
Image courtesy of Jim Kennard

My "shipwreck" searching did not end with our failed effort to find the HMS *Ontario*. For the next five years, I assisted the New York State police in searches for aircraft, trucks, and boats that went down with occupants in

Lakes Ontario, George, Champlain, the Hudson River, a reservoir, and several of the New York Finger Lakes. I also assisted a group of Canadian divers and researchers in locating an old schooner in Lake Champlain and, a few years later, found several boats in the Richelieu River in Canada for them as well. During this period, I became a manufacturer's representative for Klein Associates for all the states and Canadian provinces bordering the Great Lakes promoting their side-scan sonar products. Sometimes I conducted a side-scan survey for geophysical survey companies who were potential customers. When they were ready to purchase a system, it was a Klein side-scan sonar they chose.

In 1979, the US Army Corps of Engineers asked me to come down to Kentucky, 60 miles northeast of Louisville, to assist them in locating 24 missing barges that had broken loose in an ice floe and crashed into Markland Dam. I found all the barges in that area plus eight more that had been lost in prior years. They eventually ended up buying a Klein side-scan to assist in the salvage efforts of the barges. I guessed word of my success with the Army Corps spread because during the 1980s, four or five times a year, I helped various river transportation companies in locating their sunken barges in both the Mississippi and Ohio Rivers. My underwater searching during these years was not limited to commercial work, as my passion for discovering shipwrecks still burned bright. I made friends with divers Craig Hampton and Donny Mulhman from Lorain, Ohio, and began getting together with them to search for shipwrecks in Lake Erie. In 1980, we discovered the steamship *Morning Star* and two years later the charred remains of the *Rosa Jane*, a 46-foot luxury yacht. Back in Lake Ontario, I teamed up with Richard Nagel to discover my first shipwreck, the passenger and freight steamer *Ellsworth* that burned just off Stoney Island in 1877. Richard would join me later for more search adventures in Lake Champlain.

In these early years, there weren't many side-scan sonar systems in the world, perhaps fewer than 200. Having a side-scan gave a shipwreck hunter a tremendous advantage, but in the open waters of Lake Ontario, it was still difficult to maintain an effective and accurate search grid because there was no GPS and LORAN-C system to track your progress. As a certified SCUBA diver, I joined a dive club in Rochester and found several of their members willing to come out with me to search for shipwrecks. Most of them expected that after an hour or so of searching we would find a shipwreck and then dive on it. Hardly any of them had the patience to spend long hours, days, and weeks searching. Many of the club members were actually more interested in partying than diving and the club disbanded near

My Journey of Discovery

Scott Hill and Jim Kennard circa 1980s.   Image courtesy of Jim Kennard

the end of the 70s. At the last meeting of the club, I was showing a slide presentation about the use of side-scan sonar technology when one of the club members introduced me to Scott Hill, a diver, police officer, and avid photographer. Scott was so impressed with what he saw that evening that he contacted me later to discuss getting together the following year to search for shipwrecks.

Scott and I are both recreational divers, so we concentrated our searches in areas where we could dive on a shipwreck if we could find it. We searched in the New York Finger Lakes of Canandaigua, Seneca, Cayuga, and Keuka and found nearly 30 canal boats, barges, and a Chris Craft boat. Later, Lake Champlain would become our shipwreck playground. For a time, we were locating a new shipwreck just about every possible weekend after making the five-hour drive. The pinnacle of our success had to be our discovery in 1983 of a very early horse-powered ferryboat. In February 1989, we were invited to assist in a *National Geographic* expedition to Lake Champlain to locate a lost Revolutionary War gunboat. On that trip, we took the team to the site of the horse-powered ferryboat, which had sunk off shore of Burlington, Vermont. They deployed a remote operated vehicle to video the shipwreck. A nine-page article about the ferryboat appeared in the October 1989 issue of *National Geographic*.

By the mid 80s, Scott and I had covered most of the recreational dive areas in the lakes we were searching. Scott was very busy with his new job as Commander of the Rochester Police SCUBA Squad and I was busy

Jim Kennard diving on a shipwreck in Seneca Lake. Image courtesy of Scott Hill

spending more time with my sons in Scouts and Little League baseball. My sonar wasn't being utilized. A Midwest diver, Jack O'Keefe, offered to buy my side-scan sonar system and I felt it was time to let it go. Over the next 10 years, Jack used the side-scan from time to time in the Great Lakes, off the California coast, and in the Caribbean. By the mid-90s, the system was not getting much use and had become corroded from the salty ocean air. During a trip back north, Jack asked me to repair the unit and then let me borrow it for searches until he returned to pick it up. Jack never came back for it and I went back out with friends in Lake Champlain and Lake Erie over the next few summers.

Always looking for new people to partner with on long shipwreck exploration efforts, early in 2002, I visited a local dive shop to inquire if the owner was interested in getting together for shipwreck searching in Lake Ontario. He was too busy with his shop but suggested that a young local technical diver might be interested. Technical diving is not the same as recreational diving. With specialized equipment and training, technical divers can go well beyond the 130-foot-depth limit set for recreational divers. That day the stars must have aligned because five minutes later, the diver, Dan Scoville, entered the store. We chatted about diving in the lake and about the capabilities of the side-scan. In another month or so we got together to look for a couple of canal boats that had sunk in Seneca Lake. We found them and Dan made the dive to video the shipwreck with an underwater camera that he had borrowed from the dive shop owner. With

Dan's ability to dive deep, we now had an opportunity to find shipwrecks in Lake Ontario in depths of 250 feet or less. Searching on Lake Ontario, my original dream, could now commence in earnest. What Dan and I, and later, Roland Stevens and Roger Pawlowski were able to find and identify seems almost unbelievable as I look back over the past years. But with those memories of success, come the memories of trial and tribulation, of hours spent on the water and money spent from the pocket. It has not been easy.

Over the years, our strategy for finding shipwrecks has remained fairly constant. We research the loss of a particular ship, establish a search grid, and go hunting. Sometimes we find that ship in the search area, but often we have to expand the search area: we have learned, sometimes, those initial reports of the location are not as accurate as hoped. Occasionally, serendipity strikes and we find other unexpected wrecks in that search grid. The process of identifying a discovered shipwreck is not complicated. Unfortunately, name boards and names painted on the stern rarely provide confirmation of a ship's identity. In my experience, I have never come across a shipwreck with those clues still in existence. In a nutshell, it really is the process of elimination. First we ask the question, what ships have been reported lost in this area? Second we measure the wreck. Measurements taken by the side-scan sonar and the sector sonar on an ROV (remotely operated vehicle) allow us to match potential losses with the wreck we are investigating. Lastly, characteristics found on the wreck that we can see with video are then tested against potential identities and data gleaned from the accounts of loss. If there were survivors, or witnesses to the loss from other ships, their reports often help explain details that are found on the wreck site.

Although the process has remained constant over the years, the technology has improved dramatically. My home-built side-scan sonar slowly became obsolete. The paper for the recorder was in very limited supply and did not have a long shelf life. For several years, I had been communicating online with Fredrik Elmgren in Sweden who was interested in developing an interface to save older side-scan sonar systems from becoming totally useless. After a few years, he decided it would be much better to develop a new high-resolution side-scan sonar system that was compatible with a laptop computer and soon afterward the *DeepVision SE* side-scan sonar company was formed. In 2009, one of the company owners, Uffe Långström, flew to the US and brought me an early design of their side-scan sonar system that they had just begun to sell. We tested the side-scan in the St. Lawrence and Hudson Rivers and it worked extremely well capturing high-resolution sonar images on the laptop computer display screen. No more paper recordings. This came just in time and now, nine years later with the discovery of many more shipwrecks, the *DeepVision* side-scan sonar system is still working well.

Improvements in side-scan sonar technology have been important, but unless you can tow the side-scan out into the lake, those improvements mean nothing. For years we have used my 18-foot bowrider to conduct searches. As we went further and further from shore, my boat was just too small to be out that far and had little room to move around among a sonar system, tow cable, and dive gear. Dan bought a much larger boat, which we used until he moved to the Houston area. Roger Pawlowski, whom I had worked with at Harris Corporation, expressed an interest in being involved in the search for sunken shipwrecks. Roger is a diver and had a boat that was big enough for both dive and search equipment. In 2011, Roger joined our team. Roger not only provided us with a boat but he decided to purchase a *VideoRay Pro IV* remote operated vehicle to capture the video images of ships in deep water. When Dan relocated to the Houston area, we also lost the use of the ROV he designed and developed at Rochester Institute of Technology. Roger's participation in our later efforts helped to fill that void. Since deploying an ROV on a shipwreck, first with Dan and later with Roger, the team has been helped tremendously by Roland Stevens who joined the team in 2005. As an artist, Roland uses the underwater video of the shipwreck to create a full image of the shipwreck as it appears on the bottom. Because we have found so many shipwrecks at very deep depths, even with onboard lighting or a light dropped above a shipwreck, it is next to impossible to get an image of the shipwreck it its entirety. Roland, with his superior technical skills as an artist, makes that happen.

I have spent in some capacity, the last 40 or so years looking for shipwrecks. It has been an exciting adventure for me and I hope for those I've met along the way or who have participated in some manner in these discoveries. With a little luck, the journey will continue for years to come. Join us. You can follow our discoveries and those of other explorers on the website: www.shipwreckworld.com

Jim Kennard

Where Shipwrecks are Located in Lake Ontario

Lake Ontario was first seen by a European in 1615 by French explorer Étienne Brûlé. Sixty-three years later, in 1678, the explorer La Salle intensified his quest to conquer the heart of the continent by building a small barque he named *Frontenac*. In the fall of that year this vessel became the first sailing ship to carry men and building materials across Lake Ontario from what is now Canada to the mouth of the Niagara River. The next year the *Frontenac* became the first ship lost on Lake Ontario when she wrecked in a storm near shore about 30 miles east of Niagara. Since that time, over 340 years, many ships have been lost in the lake. Over the past 40 years, I have studied published monographs, original newspaper accounts, government documents, and insurance records and have concluded that over 600 ships sank, wrecked, burned or were scuttled in the lake, but only a portion still exist on the lake bottom. Many of the ships were wrecked on shore or at the dock and a number of them caught fire and burned, so there is not much left to find or see of them. After sinking some were removed completely. I estimate that there are approximately 200 ships that still remain in Lake Ontario today. To give you a general idea of where these ships ended their final voyage I've divided the lake into 5 sections. Four of these areas are less than 100 meters (330 ft.) in depth and the fifth is the mid lake area that ranges from 100 meters to a depth of 244 meters (805 ft.). West of Rochester, New York off the southern shore of Lake Ontario are 8% of the sunken ships that have wrecked (Area A). Here the lake drops off very quickly into deep depths just a few miles from shore. Most of the remaining shipwrecks can only be visited by technical divers. Along the north shore from Burlington to Presqu'ile Point near Brighton, Ontario, are another 8% (Area B). A number of them happened off the Toronto area. The area off the north shore of Lake Ontario between Presqu'ile Point and the St. Lawrence River contains nearly 36% of the ships either sunk or wrecked (Area C). A good mix of recreational and technical diving is found in this area. The area east of Rochester all the way up to the St. Lawrence River contains 14% of sunken ship disasters (Area D). The middle area of Lake Ontario where the depths are beyond reasonable technical diving contains 34% of the remaining shipwrecks (Area E). There are four recreational dive accessible ships off Oswego and two near Pultneyville that are detailed in this book. Almost all of the others are in much deeper water.

This book details 35 shipwrecks that have been discovered in the United States waters of Lake Ontario. Below is a list of those shipwrecks and the area in which they were found.

Shipwrecks of Lake Ontario: A Journey of Discovery

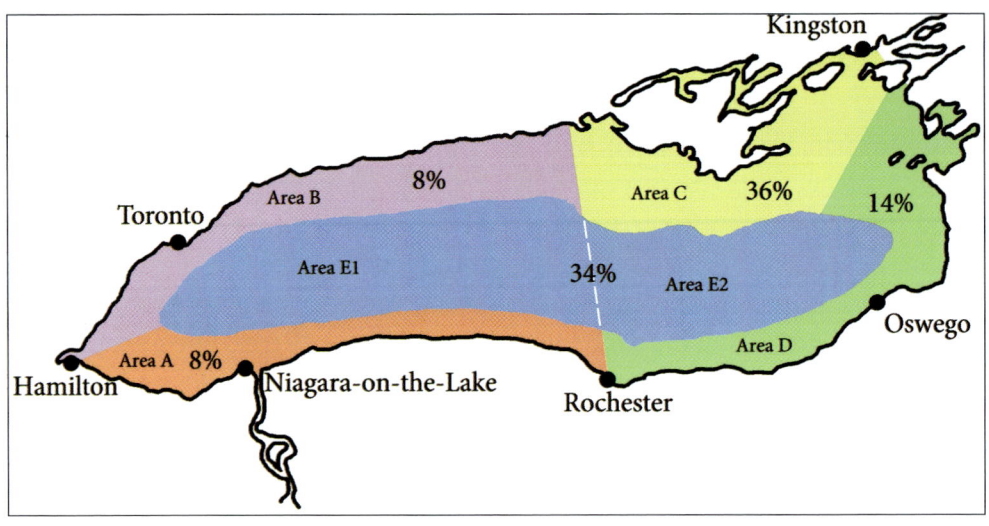

Lake Ontario divided into five areas showing percentage of all shipwrecks in each area.

Western Sector – Area A
Milan
Samuel Hodge

Eastern Sector – Area D
Atlas
Bay State
Canal Boat
Cormorant
David W. Mills
Ellsworth
Etta Bell
Harborfest Houseboat
Hartford
Homer Warren
Mary Kay
Ocean Wave
Orcadian
Queen of the Lakes
Roberval
Royal Albert
St Peter
Three Brothers
USAF C45
USCG Cable boat *CG-56022*
Washington
W. Y. Emery

Mid-Lake Sector (west) – Area E1 (over 330 ft.)
C. Reeve
HMS *Ontario*
Nisbet Grammer
Unidentified dagger-board schooner

Mid-Lake Sector (east) – Area E2 (over 330 ft.)
Black Duck
Canal Scow
Chug-A-Lug
E-Zee CRUZ'N
Issac G. Jenkins
Sea Rover
William Elgin

The Early Years
1980–2007

MY FIRST DISCOVERY ON LAKE ONTARIO: THE STEAMER *ELLSWORTH*

In the summer of 1980, my friend Richard Nagel invited me to his summer home on Point Peninsula. One of his elderly neighbors had lived on Stoney Island and had mentioned that there was a sunken ship just off shore on the east side of the island. As a young boy, his neighbor recalled, he would swim out to the wreck when part of a railing could be seen protruding above the water. He thought that it was a tour boat or something like that which had burned at the dock many years ago. Richard and I set out in his boat with my home built side-scan sonar to try to locate the shipwreck. It did not take long to find it. The sonar showed just the bottom of the ship to the turn of the bilge. I suited up in diving gear to check it out. The first thing I saw were the huge propeller blades. I followed the shaft forward until it ended abruptly. The engine was gone. I moved up the middle of the wreck, all the time sifting through the silt for any interesting artifacts but mostly found burnt pieces of wood. I do recall seeing what appeared to be a ladder or part of a railing in the middle of the wreck. Then, buried in the mud, were the remains of a small parlor stove. On a second dive I came across a couple of rusted grappling hooks. As I recall, the wreck lay in about 20 feet of water and was probably not more than 100 yards from shore.

There are no known images of the *Ellsworth* before she burned, this is a side-scan sonar image.
Image courtesy of Tim Caza

When I began searching for shipwrecks on Lake Champlain in the 1970s and 1980s, I developed a deep appreciation for maritime history. Since I have lived a stone's throw from Lake Ontario for much of my life, I found myself developing strong connections to Great Lakes history. Years ago, I began collecting information on ship sinkings in Lake Ontario from both primary and secondary sources. It took a long time, and the work still continues today, but my database, with over 600 ships that have wrecked, sunk, or were destroyed by fire in Lake Ontario, has played a critical role in determining search grids and confirming the identity of targets we find. When it came to the shipwreck east of Stoney Island, I found reference in the *Oswego Daily Palladium* from July 1877 to the burning of the steamer *Ellsworth*, exactly where Richard and I had found it.

The *Ellsworth* was originally built as a schooner-rigged canal boat in 1869 on Seneca Lake. The intent was to operate the boat on several of the New York Finger Lakes and canals from New York to Canada without the need to offload cargo to another form of transportation. With hinged masts, she could pass under bridges while navigating through the canals. In 1870, Abner C. Mattoon purchased the vessel and refitted her with steam the next year, with a boiler from the tug *Dodge*. In November 1872, the steamer departed Oswego and spent a year on the east coast delivering a variety of cargoes to places like Virginia and North Carolina. In 1873, the *Ellsworth* returned to Oswego to carry on the freight business from that port. In 1873, 25 feet were added to the former sailing vessel making the steamer *Ellsworth* 123 feet in length in order to be more effective in the barley trade. Her beam measured 17 feet 6 inches with a hold depth of 8 ½ feet. Mattoon installed double arches that extended from bow to stern and her timbers were doubled throughout, to improve her overall strength and to decrease the severity of hogging. The carrying capacity of the *Ellsworth* was estimated to be 10,000 bushels of wheat. Mattoon intended to run her between the ports of Oswego, Detroit, and Cleveland, as well as an occasional trip to the east coast.

In mid-July 1877, Abner C. Mattoon, owner of the Ellsworth, took a break from his freight and passenger business for a 10-day vacation with his family and several friends to cruise eastern Lake Ontario and the islands in the St. Lawrence River aboard his vessel. The party left Oswego on July 10, for Stoney Island located at the northeast end of the lake. Upon arrival, most of the party went off to set up camp on the island for the night. Mattoon, the captain, engineer, and steward remained aboard. Later in the evening, the captain and engineer took a small boat and rowed to land to gather bait from a nearby minnow pond. Mattoon and the steward turned in for the night to their respective cabins. Around 10 p.m., they were aroused by a fisherman shouting, "Fire! Fire!" The fisherman furiously rowed out from shore towards the burning ship. Mattoon woke up to a smoke-filled cabin and quickly hurried to the galley in the aft end of the boat where the fire appeared to have originated. Mattoon appraised the situation as hopeless, and returned to the wheelhouse to collect his important books and papers. He grabbed the compass, a hatchet, and his marine glasses, only to discover later that it was just the empty case. The fire and smoke spread rapidly forcing him to abandon his ship, leaving the important books and papers to the destructive flames. Both the steward and Mattoon escaped the burning ship in one of the small boats on board. The fire raged on for the next four hours until the *Ellsworth* sank in 21 feet of water. The light from the burning steamer could be seen for miles. The cause of the fire has never been determined. Later, newspapers reported that the belongings of the excursionists that still remained had since been recovered. Mattoon was able to secure a sailboat to get to Sackets Harbor and then returned to Oswego by train. The *Ellsworth* was insured for $7,500, about 75 percent of its total value.

In June 1879, a salvage operation commenced at Stoney Island in an effort to raise the steamer. The operation was only partly successful. The hull of the ship broke in half during the operation and Mattoon allowed it to sink again to the bottom of the lake. Later Mattoon decided to salvage the engine, which was raised piece by piece. The engine and gear were installed in the new steam barge *Thompson Kingsford* built for Mattoon in 1880.

As my first Lake Ontario shipwreck discovery, the *Ellsworth* momentarily satisfied a desire to locate and dive on a wreck to see it as it existed over 140 years ago. Attempting to identify the shipwreck brought out its fascinating history, which only increased my appreciation for the role research would play in future discoveries.

SOURCES:

Oswego Daily Palladium, November 25, 1872.
_____, October 9, 1873.
_____, July 11, 1877.
_____, July 12, 1877.
_____, July 19, 1877.
_____, May 20, 1879.
Oswego Daily Times, October 9, 1873.

ST PETER

By Bob Bristol

On October 5, 1898, the *St Peter* left Toledo, Ohio, on the first leg of her last voyage. She was a 135-foot three-masted schooner built in her homeport of Toledo in 1873. On that October day, she carried a load of corn from Toledo bound for Kingston, Ontario. She unloaded in Kingston and sailed empty to Oswego, New York arriving on October 21. In Oswego, the ship was loaded with 607 tons of chestnut coal. A fully loaded schooner would have a freeboard of two feet or less. The *St Peter* was towed into the lake at 7 a.m., Wednesday, October 26, just missing a report from Chicago that a blizzard with 70 miles per hour winds was coming their way. Her crew consisted of Captain John Griffin, his wife Josephine, first mate John McCrate, and three Swedish immigrants working for passage west.

Four miles from the safety of the Niagara River at 10:30 p.m. the storm struck with full force. Captain Griffin had no choice but to turn back east and run with the storm. The *St Peter* sailed east and displayed a burning torch as it sailed by Charlotte, New York. The torch signaled they were asking for tug services to pull them from the lake. The U.S. Lifesaving Service responded by sending out the *Proctor*, a 110-foot tugboat, to tow their men in a skiff out onto the lake. From 4 a.m. to daylight they searched the lake with no success. They returned to the Genesee River and were just sitting down to breakfast when a report came in that a schooner was flying a distress signal off Bear Creek in the town of Ontario, New York.

The tug *Proctor* was used once again to tow the lifesavers in their skiff down the lake toward the distressed schooner. The storm had increased in strength to gale force winds. One report from the lifesavers in the skiff had them losing sight of the smokestack on the *Proctor* because of the wave heights. Since the *Proctor* was a 110-foot boat, I estimate that the wave heights were probably 25 feet.

At approximately 11 a.m., the crew on the *Proctor* sighted the *St Peter* through the troughs of the waves inshore from their position. They steamed toward the schooner and were horrified to see it give a lurch to port followed by a second and then it disappeared. Once on scene they rescued a man hanging onto a pair of skiff oars. There was no sighting of other survivors in the water. The *St Peter* had been underway for 28 hours and traveled some 240 miles since leaving Oswego only to sink off Fairbanks Point in the town of Williamson, New York. The lone survivor turned out to be Captain John Griffin. He stated that he saw his wife Josephine and the entire crew in the water. He believed his wife lasted longer than the men. The *Proctor* continued running east with the storm to Sodus Point, New York. As a side story, the lifesavers retrieved the skiff oars Captain Griffin used to keep himself afloat.

Final resting place of the *St Peter*.
Image courtesy of Teddy Garlock

The Rochester Coast Guard crew found them again in 1935 while cleaning out a cart building at the station. Although I located the wife of the *Rochester Democrat and Chronicle* reporter who detailed the story of the skiff oars in 1935, my search for the oars hit a dead end and today, the oars remain lost to history.

In 1968, my dive partner Tom Mulhall learned of "an old shipwreck from the last century" that might be off Fairbanks Point. A college department head who lived near the point was the source of the information. Tom and other shipwreck hunters spent time searching for the wreck in the 1968 and 1969 dive season, but sadly had no success. For me it all started in 1970 when I launched *Deepstar 1*, a restored 26-foot, 1947 Steelcraft motorboat, which served as my search vessel and dive boat operating out of Hughes Marina in Williamson, New York. Our plan was to search the area using the chart recording depth sounder on *Deepstar 1*. This was minimal equipment given what is available today. Essentially, to locate a shipwreck, we had to run right across the top of it and record the significant change in depth. Worse yet, at the time, there was no LORAN and GPS to help you maintain an effective grid search.

On August 14, 1970, I changed a fuel pump on one of the engines in the old Steelcraft and took the boat out alone to test things out. At 10:30 p.m., it was a nice night on the lake, calm with an offshore breeze. I shut the engines down and drifted. I turned on the depth sounder from time to time noting it was getting deeper each time. At a depth of 110 feet and approximately two miles off shore I noted a lot of fish showing on the chart. Suddenly I drifted over this object which was 15 feet taller than the bottom, as indicated on the chart recorder. I just found something "big." I wondered, however, if I could relocate this spot again in daylight. Navigation at the

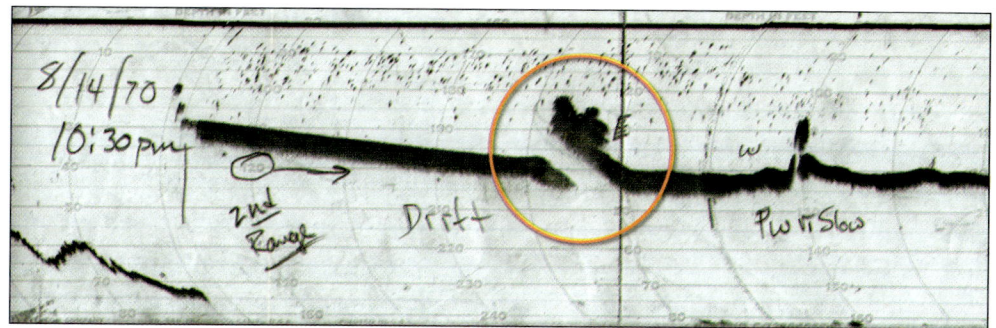

This depth graph is the actual recording of depth when the *St Peter* was discovered on August 14, 1970. Image courtesy of Bob Bristol

time was compass, depth sounder and visual reference. Using the depth, direction and angle to the light at the entrance to Hughes Marina, I was able to relocate the object the next day. I called my dive partner Tom Mulhall Sunday afternoon and told him what I found. We chatted all week and organized a dive for the next weekend to investigate the target. After some difficulty relocating the spot, four divers went down the anchor line in cold and murky water to find a ship lying on the bottom.

In 1971, we applied for and received a New York State Permit issued jointly by the New York State Department of Education (History) and the Office of General Services (State underwater land ownership) to dive and recover artifacts on behalf of the Pultneyville Historical Society which promised to preserve the recovered artifacts.

We dived the *St Peter* every chance we could. We pumped water down from the surface to clear mud and debris away. We brought many artifacts up but the most significant recovery of the year was the ship's wheel and gearbox. From the damage at the stern, it appears the *St Peter* struck the bottom stern first breaking away the rudder and transom. This left the wheel and gearbox

St Peter's recovered wheel. Image courtesy of Bob Bristol

exposed. The assembly was made by the Boston Machine Co. We used float bags to lift the assembly to the surface.

In the summer of 1972, we continued bringing up more artifacts. It was a difficult job because it was dark on the shipwreck, a cold 37 degrees, and the visibility was a foot or two using lights. Because the visibility was so poor, it took a while to discover the boards in one area of the aft deck didn't align with the other deck boards. We were looking at the cabin roof which had collapsed on the deck. The broken mizzen mast was sticking six feet through the collapsed roof.

We decided to remove the roof, an effort which almost sunk our boat. With a line tied onto the roof and the other end onto our boat, we pulled the roof up and over the stub of the broken mizzen mast and sailed it off the left side of the ship. Once the weight of the roof caught up with us, the stern of our boat started to go under. We had a knife at the ready and cut the line averting another shipwreck.

From the reports after the *St Peter* sinking, we learned Captain Griffin's daughter hired a hard hat diver in 1899 to go down to find her mother and a purse containing money. The diver had to descend through the still standing rigging to the deck to search the cabin. We found large rounded rocks in the main mast area. The diver most likely used these to help his descent to the deck. He reported seeing the overturned cabin stove but no purse with money the daughter was seeking. When we looked at the cabin 73 years later, the stove was still turned over. The main mast was a navigational hazard as it stuck out of water by eight feet so a few years after the sinking it was lifted and pulled over. The bottom of the mast now rests on the port railing.

In 1973, we decided to retrieve the starboard anchor. The anchor had been hanging off the bow. We cut the anchor chain in 1972, which took about six dives using a hacksaw. Each single tank dive gave a diver less than 20 minutes on the deck. I estimated the anchor weighed 1,800 pounds. The lifting process involved using a 275-gallon household heating oil tank cabled to the anchor. We filled the tank from the surface using 10 scuba tanks of air. It was a gentle process. Once the divers confirmed the oil tank was upright and ready to take the load, we continued filling the tank. The anchor was buried in the mud and didn't want to come up. A tug with the *Deepstar 1* broke it free from the bottom. The lake was flat calm that day, August 7. At 12:47 p.m. the tank arrived at the surface in one big bulging bubble, having had expelled three and a half times its volume of air due to the pressure differences. We towed the tank and anchor into about 30 feet of water. We re-rigged the tank to the anchor so it didn't draw as much water, then brought the whole package into Hughes Marina. With the help of Milo, a local mechanic, and his tow truck, the anchor was brought out of the water for the first time in 75 years. The anchor is currently located at Hughes Marina.

In the summer of 1974, there were fewer dives due to rough weather but we still brought up

St Peter's anchor hauled to the surface.
Image courtesy of Bob Birstol

some interesting artifacts. In that year, we recovered mostly items from the cabin and lazarette area where tools were stored. The one interesting find was the ship's bell, which was a cast iron farm type of bell made by the Gould Pump company in Seneca Falls, New York. As an interesting side story, while enjoying a bonfire on the beach after a day of diving, I took the bell out of the trunk of my car and rang it. A light in the corner of the marina went out. Everybody thought it was Josephine's ghost turning out the light. It turned out to be faulty wiring.

Crew of the *Deepstar 1* just hanging out on the recovered anchor.   Image courtesy of Bob Bristol

The artifacts were generally in good condition. The lack of light and 37-degree water preserved leather shoes and even a crock of cheese. The cheese smelled bad but we were told by the Rochester Museum and Science Center that it was still edible. Incredibly, potato skins came to the surface after clearing the cabin.

In 1975, the Rochester Museum and Science Center produced an exhibit and book called "It was a Dark and Stormy Night." The exhibit told the story of the *St Peter*, our diving, and displayed artifacts recovered from the shipwreck. We worked with Dick Kilday and the museum staff to provide needed information and artifacts. The exhibit was on display in the New York State Capitol, the Wayne County Museum in Lyons, New York, and currently is with the Pultneyville Historical Society and Museum in Pultneyville, New York.

Summer 1977 saw the last of our diving crew on the *St Peter*. For 7 years, 16 divers spent hundreds of man hours each locating and salvaging the *St Peter*. We endured the cold temperatures and darkness. Only two experienced divers suffered a case of the bends and had to go to the decompression chamber in Buffalo, New York for treatment. In March 2004, the *St Peter* was placed on the National Register of Historic Places.

Fallen mast of the *St Peter*.
Image courtesy of Teddy Garlock

Today the occasional diver sees zebra mussels covering the wreck. The mussel's filtering of the water has increased the visibility to 80+ feet. For me, when I want to return to the days of diving the *St Peter*, I go virtual and view the video clips on YouTube.com.[1]

Bob Bristol grew up in Vermont and is now a retired engineer living in Matlacha, Florida. Growing up on Lake Champlain, he was intrigued by what lies below. His first scuba dive was in 1960 which kindled his keen interest in diving. Schooling and work brought him to the Rochester, New York area. Discovering the St Peter is one of the highlights of his many varied experiences.

---

[1] The *St Peter* is found at N 43° 18.690' W 77° 07.812'

LAST VOYAGE OF THE STEAMER *HOMER WARREN*

Steamer *Homer Warren*.   Image courtesy of the Great Lakes Historical Society Collection of the Historical Collection of the Great Lakes at Bowling Green State University

Soon after Dan Scoville and I teamed up, we read about the *Homer Warren* tragedy and decided to try to locate this specific steamer. We first reviewed local newspapers from October 1919 for accounts of the disaster. Using this research, we estimated the probable search area based on several factors: the sighting of the ship, time of the sinking, wind direction, drift rate, and the location of the debris. In 2002, we began searching using my home-built side-scan sonar and covered nearly 30 square miles of Lake Ontario without success. In early June 2003, we returned to the area and within a few weeks were rewarded with a potential target we thought might be the steamship *Homer Warren*. We were a few miles off the southern shore of Lake Ontario near Pultneyville, New York. The sonar record clearly showed an image of a ship the shape and size of the *Homer Warren*. Off to one side of the ship there appeared to be several large pieces of debris. We were hopeful that we had found her.

Using mixed gases, necessary for the extreme depth, Dan made a dive to the shipwreck to document and identify other characteristics that would help confirm this was indeed the *Homer Warren*. Dan made several additional dives with a video camera to document the condition of the vessel at its resting place on the lake bottom. The ship is upright. Both of the cabins

Boiler from the *Homer Warren*, with diver Teddy Garlock. Image courtesy of Jill Heinerth

Debris from the *Homer Warren*, with diver Teddy Garlock. Image courtesy of Jill Heinerth

and main deck are missing, allowing access to the cargo and engine areas. Large boilers, pipes, and debris rest about 25 feet from the starboard side of the ship. This is the debris we saw on the sonar image. The steeple compound engine is partially visible through the twisted pipes and wreckage of the stern section. The ship's propeller is not visible as it is buried beneath the wreck. Both sides of the ship are covered with quagga mussels giving it the appearance of a wall of shells. At the bow, the stem rises up from the bottom almost 30 feet, like an accusing finger pointing toward the surface of Lake Ontario. A few feet back from the bow, the starboard side of the ship is pushed out and a large portion is missing. This rupture probably caused the steamer to sink rapidly during the storm.

Two years later, we surveyed the general area where the *Homer Warren* foundered. Using a new, Imagenex Yellow Fin high-resolution sonar, our survey detected a trail of debris from the wreck site further out into the lake for approximately a quarter of a mile. The entire crew was lost in the accident, so we have no firsthand accounts of that evening. Based upon what we found on the lake bottom, I theorized that heavy seas caused by strong northwest winds gradually tore the steamer apart, leaving debris

Bow of the *Homer Warren*, with diver Teddy Garlock. Image courtesy of Jill Heinerth

along the way. The *Warren*'s engines probably failed as water poured into the ship's hold making it impossible to navigate in the storm. At this point the steamer would likely have been forced broadside to the wind and waves. As pounding waves broke over the length of the ship, the upper structure of the steamer would have become unstable, eventually giving way to the seas. The deck would eventually follow the upper structure along with portions of the ship's hull causing the steamer to finally sink beneath the waves.

The newspaper accounts reported that four bodies were found on shore near the lifeboat. They were all wearing life jackets, but had apparently died from the harsh elements. The rest of the crew were never recovered and probably went down with the ship. In the deep water where the *Homer Warren* sank, a body does not rise to the surface.

On October 28, 1919, the *Homer Warren* was one of the oldest, wooden straight deck bulk freighters in operation on the Great Lakes having been built in Cleveland in 1863. The steamship departed Oswego bound for Toronto, Canada, early in the morning with a crew of nine men and a cargo of 500 tons of coal. It wasn't long before the steamer ran into heavy seas and gale force winds from the northwest. We believe the *Warren* followed the southern shoreline past Little Sodus Bay and Sodus Point then headed out into the lake. The winds steadily increased to over 60 miles per hour as she steamed into the open waters of Lake Ontario. About 10 o'clock in the morning, a fisherman near Pultneyville, New York, briefly observed a ship in trouble with heavy seas breaking over her from bow to stern. He couldn't

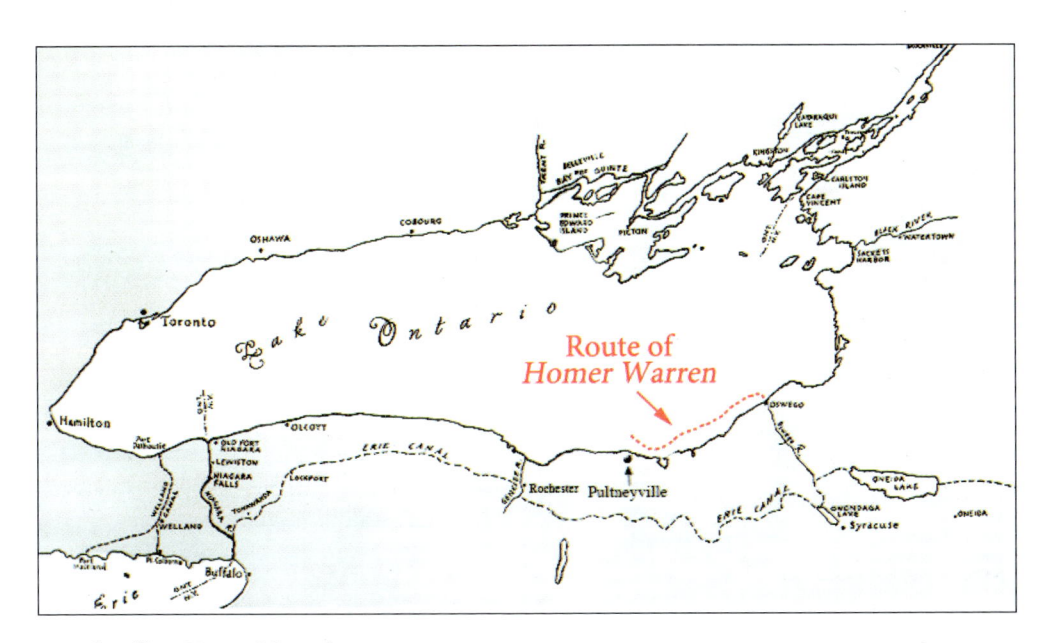

Map detailing *Homer Warren*'s course.

see the ship clearly as it was several miles from shore so he hurried home for his field glasses. When he returned, he was no longer able to locate the vessel.

Throughout the day pieces of the pilothouse and cabin, as well as trunks, bedding, a refrigerator, and other articles from the ship, washed ashore for a stretch of six miles. Oars and a lifeboat with a large hole punched in its side were found along the Pultneyville beach near the bodies of four of the crewmembers. The men were wearing life jackets and probably had taken to the small lifeboat. All perished from exposure to the cold waters of Lake Ontario. A wrist watch on one of the crew had stopped at 10 a.m. providing the most likely time of the sinking of the *Homer Warren*. The fierce gale that took the steamer to the bottom was one of the worst storms to hit the area in over 25 years. One crewmember's story is that of horrific tragedy and, yet, extreme luck.

William Kerr was the chief marine engineer and a shareholder of the *Homer Warren*. Kerr had traveled from Oswego to Toronto by rail earlier in the week. His return to Oswego was delayed and, upon learning by wire that the steamer had left for Toronto, he remained in that port to catch up with the crew and vessel there, a circumstance that ultimately saved his life. But his survival was tainted by the loss of both of his brothers who were part of the crew of the doomed ship. The bodies of the four crewmembers that washed ashore were all bruised, especially their faces, probably battered on the rocky shore in the heavy seas. The majority owners of the *Homer Warren* sent Kerr and J.P. Milne, to Sodus, New York, to identify the bodies. Kerr and Milne identified George Stalker, Joseph Kerr, George Kerr, and Patrick Howe, all members of the *Warren*'s crew.

The crew of the *Homer Warren*:

William Stalker, Captain — Penetang, Ontario
George Stalker, Mate and brother of captain — Penetang, Ontario
Joseph Kerr, Second Engineer — Toronto, Ontario
George Kerr, Fireman and brother of Joseph — Toronto, Ontario
Stanley Foster, Deckhand — Toronto, Ontario
William Talbot, Deckhand — Oswego, New York
Patrick Howe, Cook — Oswego, New York
Thompson, Deckhand — Port Hope, Ontario
Unknown man, Deckhand

The loss of the *Homer Warren* is probably one of Lake Ontario's most well-known disasters. The research process that created our search grid to find her also opened up to me the rich history of the vessel before it sank. The steamer *Homer Warren* was originally built as the *Atlantic* by Peck and Masters of Cleveland, Ohio, in 1863. The steamer was built to carry freight and passengers for the New York Central Railroad and was run by the railroad and its subsidiaries for the next four years. In 1867, the *Atlantic* was acquired by Cleveland Transportation Company, then sold to the Union Steamboat Transportation Company in 1869. During its ownership, the ship had a new main deck installed as well as new arches. In 1882, S.B. Grummond acquired the vessel. Under Grummond, she continued carrying passengers and package freight serving as effective competition to the Detroit and Cleveland Navigation Company. Besides typical repairs initiated during Grummond's ownership, the *Atlantic* had a new electric plant installed and more importantly, the bow was sheathed in boiler iron. This helped protect the ship in icy conditions.

In 1896, the *Atlantic* was sold to H. S. Brown and remained in his family for five years. A fire in late August 1899 partially destroyed the ship. The *Detroit Free Press* newspaper noted that the *Atlantic* was "but a mere skeleton of her former self." The ship was overhauled at Davidson Shipyard in West Bay City in 1899 and fitted out as a lumber hooker with a new steeple compound engine from Montague Works in Benton Harbor, Michigan. In 1901, Frank Andrews acquired the ship and renamed it the *Homer Warren*. The *Warren* changed hands two more times between 1901 and 1916 before the Milne brothers purchased the ship to serve their coal company which was headquartered in Toronto. In 1919, the ownership of the vessel was redistributed with 48 shares belonging to the Milne Brothers, 8 shares to Chief Engineer William Kerr, and another 8 shares to her captain, William Stalker.

The rich history of the *Homer Warren* before she sank taught me an important lesson. Not only can the history be used to help identify a shipwreck site, but this history is the context that makes our discovery not just a scientific event, but an historical one as well. When we found the *Homer Warren* in 2003, she was the first shipwreck discovered in the deep waters off the south shore of Lake Ontario that had not been salvaged. The depths of Lake Ontario in this area prevented recreational divers from attempting to find and dive these wrecks. Technical divers, like Dan, could do so, but the costs associated with such an expedition had kept efforts to a minimum. Even today, she is one of the older steamships still in existence in the Great Lakes, albeit on the bottom of Lake Ontario.

One of the nameplates from the steamer *Homer Warren* may have been retrieved from the ship's debris that came ashore in the Pultneyville/Sodus area in 1919. In 2005 we received communications from Paul Warren who

Nameboard of the *Homer Warren*. Image courtesy of Paul Warren

sent us pictures of a partial nameplate with the inscription *Homer Warren*. Warren bought it from an antique dealer in Carlisle, Pennsylvania, who acquired it from another dealer in the Jamestown, New York area. The nameplate measures approximately 6 feet long by 1½ feet wide. There was no inscription on the back of the nameplate to identify where it had been made, or when.

SOURCES:

Heyl, Eric. *Early American Steamers*. Buffalo, New York, 1953.
Rochester Democrat & Chronicle, October 30, 1919.
Record [Sodus, New York], October 31, 1919.
Rochester Herald, October 30, 1919.
Rochester Post Express, October 29, 1919.
_____, October 30, 1919.
Rochester Times Union, October 29, 1919.
_____, October 30, 1919.

In September 2018 professional underwater photographer Jill Heinerth along with Teddy Garlock made technical dives on the *Homer Warren* to capture the most recent imagery of these shipwrecks.

(A Version of this chapter was published previously in *Inland Seas*®, Summer 2007 — Volume 63 Page 126)

Lake Ontario Claims the Schooner *Etta Belle* in Calm Weather

After our discovery of the steamer *Homer Warren* in June 2003, Dan Scoville and I set our sights on finding the *Sophia*, a little sailing ship that sank in 1827 under the command of its owner, Horatio Throop of Pultneyville, New York. His ship would have been one of the oldest commercial ships that sailed on Lake Ontario and of great interest to many nautical historians in our area. The *Sophia* was en route from Pultneyville to Oswego loaded with a cargo of corn when she foundered six miles from Sodus Point. It was thought that the corn she carried may have swelled up due to a leak causing the hull to breach, rapidly sending the *Sophia* to the bottom of the lake. Captain Throop was the only one of the crew of three who survived after he reportedly swam four miles to shore. Our search for the *Sophia* continued throughout that summer and into the fall. After one particularly long day of searching, we got lucky. While returning to shore, the side-scan sonar was still running when an unexpected object appeared on the sonar recording paper. The image of the object was somewhat distorted because we were running fast and not towing the side-scan sonar towfish sensor close to the bottom. We turned the boat around to go back to check out the target more thoroughly only to have our engine shut down. After repeated attempts, the engine finally started but we thought it best to head back to shore before we became stranded on the lake for the night. The target looked to me like a large rock so I named it "Dan's Rock".

Over the next two months, we came to believe that "Dan's Rock" was more than just a rock and most likely an undiscovered shipwreck. The rough seas during that fall prevented our return to the target until well beyond the normal Lake Ontario boating season. In mid-November, we experienced what we call a weather window, a day of calm wind and no waves. We seized the opportunity to get back on the lake to check out "Dan's Rock." Using the side-scan sonar, we set it for a shorter range to provide more detail and confirmed our suspicions that "Dan's Rock" was in fact a shipwreck. Maybe we had found the *Sophia*! We anchored near the shipwreck. Dan got into his dry suit and strapped on his multiple tanks filled with mixed gas for the technical dive.

Dan also carried an underwater video camera to document the remains of the shipwreck. The visibility of the water at this time of year was exceptional and allowed him to see the faint outline of almost the entire length of the ship as he descended to the bottom. The video camera began to record his descent. The railings and deck of the ship appeared first, followed by a view of the ship's holds and a spare mast lying on the deck. Next came a view of the winch, a length of chain, and two large anchors. Then, the camera jammed and stopped working! At that point, the video recording of the schooner had amounted to less than one minute, but the first images of the shipwreck were absolutely spectacular. Unfortunately, it was another six months before Dan and I were able to return for his next look at this fine example of a freshwater shipwreck.

Etta Belle. Updated 2018 image courtesy of Roger Pawlowski

Etta Belle's bow. Updated 2018 image courtesy of Roger Pawlowski

During the 2004 season, we returned to the wreck to document, with video, the condition of the schooner. The ship sits evenly on the bottom with the bow slightly raised upward. Both of the ship's anchors are still firmly in place on deck at the bow. The holds are filled to capacity with coal. There are two masts; both lie on the port side of the stern having fallen away. The sails have long since disintegrated. A small cabin existed at one time that was about 10 feet long and stretched across from the starboard to port side of the ship. The roof of the cabin has collapsed onto the deck.

The ship probably sank due to a leak caused by a puncture in the side of the hull. We discovered a

Etta Belle's broken up stern. Updated 2018 image courtesy of Roger Pawlowski

four-by-six-inch hole on the port side of the schooner just one foot under the water line and four feet from the bow. The schooner appears to have gone down stern first, as there is extensive damage in the stern area.

The ship's rudder lies just under the ship's wheel along with portions of the stern railing and other debris, all having broken loose. The entire ship is encrusted with zebra and quagga mussels, but the old wooden shipwreck is still a beautiful sight to see.

At this point, we were pretty sure that this was not the *Sophia*, but some other lost vessel. Later in the season, we invited Chris Koberstein, a friend from Canada who is also a technical diver, to help us measure the target, which would help us identify the schooner. There were no records of Throop's *Sophia* that provided the ship's actual dimensions but there were tonnage estimates that would put the length in the range of around 50 feet. The ship that we discovered was over 90 feet in length. The cargo in the hold was coal — definitely not the *Sophia*, which held corn. After an intense search of published resources, we turned up a small article in the September 5, 1873 edition of the *Oswego Daily Palladium* newspaper that described the loss of the schooner *Etta Belle* off Big Sodus Bay. The *Etta Belle*'s Captain Palow stated that a leak was discovered, "on the bluff of the port bow, below the water mark and that the water rushed in in such violence that the pumps were entirely useless." This corresponded to the four-by-six-inch hole on the port side of the shipwreck that was clearly visible in the underwater video. Next, I sent for the enrollment papers for the *Etta Belle*. They confirmed that the dimensions of the ship matched the measurements made by Chris and Dan. The enrollment papers also provided some additional details relating to owners and vessel registration that helped flesh out the story.

In 1871, the schooner *Etta Belle* was rebuilt from the hull of the *Champion* that had wrecked in 1870 near Port Hope, Canada. Using the hull of a salvaged or damaged ship was common practice on the Great Lakes. When she was rebuilt, the *Etta Belle* measured 93 feet in length and had a beam of 19 feet. Her builders constructed her with oak and designed a bow with a semicircular shape which gave her the look of a barge. More importantly, this created additional space for cargo — even if it meant she was slower in the water. The owners listed her homeport as Cape Vincent, New York. Vessels of her type in the 1870s were often used to transport grain and coal on the St. Lawrence River and Lake Ontario.

The *Etta Belle* departed Little Sodus Bay at North Fair Haven for Toronto mid-afternoon on September 3, 1873, heading out into Lake Ontario in relatively calm weather. Underway only a few hours, the crew

Etta Belle's bow showing the hole on the port side.
Updated 2018 image courtesy of Roger Pawlowski

discovered that the ship was taking on water around 6 p.m. Captain Palow found a substantial leak coming from an opening somewhere in the area of the port bow and below the waterline of the schooner. The crew immediately manned the pumps in a desperate effort to save the ship and themselves. However, the flow of water into the schooner was much greater than the pumps could handle and the *Etta Belle* sank lower into the water with every passing minute. The crew continuously worked to pump water out of the hold. After an hour, the captain conceded that the schooner was going down very soon and gave the order to abandon ship. The captain and crew took to the small yawl. They rowed for the next several hours to the safety of the nearest shore, landing at Sodus Point, a distance of about eight miles. Since their quick departure from the sinking ship did not allow any time to gather their belongings, the crew arrived on land with little more than the clothes they were wearing. The captain of the *Etta Belle* stated that he believed the cause of the leak had happened while the cargo was being loaded causing the butt end of one of the narrow boards that make up the side of the schooner to come loose. He speculated that this situation probably became progressively worse as the schooner headed out and into the swells on the lake.

In 2004, the *Etta Belle* was the first discovered commercial sailing vessel that wrecked in the deep waters off the southern shore of Lake Ontario near Sodus Point, New York. Since then, we have searched and discovered others in this area, but as of 2018 the sailing ship *Sophia*, the target we initially set out to find in 2003, has yet to be discovered. However, we have not given up hope of ever finding the *Sophia*. Over the years, our shipwreck sleuthing experience has taught us that perseverance pays off. Perhaps someone reading this chapter will have a piece of information that will lead us to the final resting place of the long lost little schooner *Sophia*.

SOURCES:

Oswego Daily Palladium, September 4, 1873.
_____, September 5, 1873.

Salt Ship

The *Milan* under sail. Watercolor by Roland E. Stevens III

In the summer of 2005, Dan Scoville and I turned our sights west to spend time searching the waters off Oak Orchard, New York, 40 or so miles east of Rochester, in hopes of finding the *C. Reeve*. The newspaper account of her loss appeared to provide good details of the schooner's location, so we thought this might be an easy find. Dan and I began searching off Oak Orchard running search patterns east and west, back and forth, following latitude lines just like mowing a lawn. As the weeks and months went by, we expanded our search going farther to the east, west and then out into the lake. Our efforts revealed nothing but a flat, featureless lake bottom. Then an image of a sailing ship with the masts still standing popped up on the paper record of the side-scan sonar. Wow! The months of searching finally paid off, but was this target the schooner *C. Reeve*? The condition of the ship seemed unusual since masts typically fall off to the side of the ship or are pulled off when they are visible above water. We found this shipwrecked schooner in very deep water, well beyond the limits for recreational SCUBA divers of 130 feet and even well beyond a depth that many technical divers feel comfortable using their advanced diving skills. Due to this limitation, we had no opportunity to view our discovery up close for the remainder of the 2005 season. Dan, determined to see this wreck, led a Rochester Institute of Technology senior design project in the fall of 2005 to create a remote operated vehicle that could explore underwater, relieving us of the dangerous task of technical diving in deep water.

In 2006, we deployed the underwater remote operated vehicle (ROV) developed by Dan and his team to explore the shipwreck we found the previous season in hopes of confirming its identity as the *C. Reeve*. Equipped with a low-light, black-and-white video camera, the ROV can take video that is then transmitted to a monitor top side. The schooner is sitting evenly on the bottom with both masts still in place and rising up approximately 70 feet from the lake bottom. The masts go through the deck of the ship, which is all that keeps them in place as the rigging as well as the sails, have long since disintegrated. Deadeyes and pulley blocks are lying on the deck in various places. Just under the bowsprit there is a stem scroll, a very simple decorative feature in the place where a figurehead might appear. Both the anchors are still firmly in place on either side of the ship near the

Milan underwater. Watercolor by Roland E. Stevens III

bow with their chains wound up tightly on the windlass. There are two openings to the hold of the ship. Both hatch covers are slid back allowing entrance to the hold, which is almost completely filled with silt. A double common bilge pump is located next to the mainmast. The ship's cabin is still standing, but pieces of the roof are scattered nearby. This opening made it easy to view the interior of the cabin. Two windows are in the rear of the cabin and two smaller windows are on each side of the center companionway, although the glass in no longer present. There appears to be several feet of silt inside, but there is no evidence of the contents of the cabin except for a small cabinet, which is secured to the rear wall between the two windows. A large tiller is located at the stern of the ship, with the long handle finding its last position to the rail on the starboard side. The stern railing curves upward at its center most point. The schooner has a square stern. On the stern, the faint remains of a large raised oval decorative detail can be seen. The name of the schooner was probably painted in this area but has long since disappeared. The entire ship is encrusted with zebra and quagga mussels, but still this old wooden shipwreck is one of the most beautiful, fully intact, commercial schooners that we have seen off the shores of New York.

Once a ship is found, all efforts are made to confirm its name and history. To search for and identify a shipwreck, more time is actually spent on land — going through old newspapers on microfilm and conferring with shipwreck historians — than out on the lake in active searching. Ships that get caught in a storm often break up and the nameplate gets lost in the wreckage or the painted name on a ship ends up disappearing over time. Conducting this research prior to going out on the water is very important so you don't end up chasing after a ship that may have actually been saved or salvaged.

The side-scan sonar gave us approximate dimensions of the shipwreck we discovered. She was approximately 90 feet long and 20 feet wide. This forced us to question whether we had found the *C. Reeve*, as that vessel's documentation reported she was 120 feet in length. The schooner that we located did not have a name on the stern of the ship, but there were features that determined the probable time of construction. This schooner has a tiller. By the late 1850s, piloting by tiller had all but disappeared, replaced by full steering gear and a ship's wheel. The presence of a stem scroll (or scroll head), which is not common on the Great Lakes, can be an important factor in identifying a shipwreck.

Over the course of many months, I consulted with individuals who had developed Great Lakes shipwreck databases as well as a number of ship historians concerning the unique characteristics of this vessel. I was told the schooner *Oxford*, which sank in Lake Erie, also had a stem scroll and a tiller. The *Oxford* was built in 1848 by shipbuilder Asa Wilcox. Wilcox built a ship in 1845, prior to the *Oxford*, with many of the same characteristics, called the *Milan*. Based on the location of the target, its measurements and design characteristics, as well as the condition of the target on the lake floor, our discovery could be only one possible vessel — the schooner *Milan*.

The *Milan*'s enrollment papers provided the key link to the very similar *Oxford*. The *Milan* was built in 1845 by Asa Wilcox at Three-Mile Bay near Point Peninsula on Lake Ontario. She was a two-masted schooner with a beam of 19 feet and 8 inches, a length of 93 feet, and a square stern. The schooner *Milan* operated from 1845 to 1849. She was on record as having transported goods such as corn, flour, wheat, salt, and lumber to ports on Lake Ontario and Lake Erie.

Asa Wilcox.
Image courtesy of Kit Pitkin

On the morning of October 9, 1849, the *Milan* sailed from Oswego bound for Cleveland with a crew of nine men. She was carrying a cargo of 1,000 barrels of salt. Around 2:30 the next morning, the crew, asleep in the forecastle, was awoken by water in their sleeping area. Following normal procedure, two crewmen manned the pumps and the remaining crew began removing the salt cargo from the forward hold. Despite their efforts, the water continued to flood the ship. The captain piloted the *Milan* to the south in an effort to beach her on the southern shore of the lake. Southerly winds, however, prevented any progress. In desperation, the crew abandoned the ship and took to the yawl boat just before the *Milan* disappeared below the waves of Lake Ontario. On this last trip, the captain of the *Milan* had his dog on board and the animal seemed to go down with the ship. Miraculously, the newfoundland rose to the surface, swam to his master, and was saved. A passing schooner, the *Church*, saw the sinking and took the crew and dog onboard and brought them to the port of Rochester. Our shipwreck was found heading directly to shore and not to the nearest port. There was no observable damage to the ship, indicating that they were not in a storm or in a collision with another ship. Also the yawl was missing. These were all indications that the crew left the ship because it had devel-

The Newfoundland. Drawing by Roland E. Stevens III

oped a significant leak and was sinking fast. This matches very closely to the reported loss of the *Milan* in 1849.

With no evidence of salvage efforts or other disturbance, the *Milan* is a fantastic example of a mid-19th century Great Lakes schooner. Discovering a ship built in 1848 in near pristine condition only fueled our desire to search for even older shipwrecks. More importantly, with Dan's ROV, we proved that we could survey deep water wrecks safely with remote sensing technology. Although we have found older and perhaps more significant shipwrecks since 2006, the *Milan* remains one of my favorite discoveries. As for the *C. Reeve*, the target we thought would be "easy to find", it turned out to be more elusive than we expected and would not be discovered for a few more years.

SOURCES:

Rochester Daily Advertiser, October 12, 1849.
Rochester Republican, October 18, 1849.

The Final Chapter of
USCG Cable Boat *CG-56022*

CG-56022 above water. Image by the United States Coast Guard

Many people who consider themselves shipwreck hunters will attest to the fact that sometimes it can take decades to find a specific shipwreck. In the intervening years, perhaps new evidence is uncovered or new technology developed that can make a once-elusive, undiscoverable shipwreck, now possible to find. Two years after the sinking of a US Coast Guard cable boat (*CG-56022*) in 1977, my partner at the time, Scott Hill, and I began to look for the wreck of this cable boat using information that was printed in the local Rochester newspaper at the time of her loss. This type of boat is utilized as a floating platform to repair, remove, install, or renew various submerged cables. It is not a common boat and since it sank in 1977, it also is relatively young as a shipwreck.

Despite what appeared to be solid information, Scott and I were unsuccessful in locating *CG-56022* and felt that something was wrong, as there was no trace of the sunken boat where the newspapers reported its loss. Years later we realized that not only was the information about the boat's location inaccurate in the newspaper, but the Coast Guard itself had no idea as to the location of its own sunken vessel. In 2004, I contacted the USCG regarding

CG-56022. The reply that I received was: "This cable boat was salvaged in December 1977, then surveyed and removed from service July 17, 1978." No wonder why we couldn't find the cable boat, they salvaged it!

My friends, Bob Bristol and Tom Mulhall, remembered the cable boat's sinking. More importantly, Bob and Tom thought that the reported salvage operation actually never happened. Bristol was living at Ontario-on-the-Lake, New York in 1977 and could directly view the area of the lake where the boat went down. He and his neighbors never observed any salvage operation take place after the cable boat sank. Any salvage operation of that magnitude would have been large and lengthy — allowing locals the opportunity to remember facts about the work being done off their shore. Utilizing the search information provided by Bob and Tom, Dan and I located the final position of the cable boat with side-scan sonar on a cold and rainy day in late October 2004. When we eventually dived on the cable boat, we were very surprised at what we found.

CG-56022 landed stern first on the bottom and has remained that way, never coming to fully rest on the lake floor. It is upside down and leaning over at almost a 45-degree angle. The bow is being held upwards, buoyed by the air tanks built into the sides of the cable boat. Being a converted landing craft, the majority of the weight is concentrated in the stern. In the center of the boat there is a large reel of cable looming just overhead of any diver who penetrates into the stern section of this wreck. Over the years, 12 feet of the cable boat has sunk into the bottom. The lake currents have created an 8-foot-deep crater completely surrounding the vessel. The boat is now completely covered with zebra mussels, two inches thick in some places. On one dive we observed a large quantity of lake bass congregating around the shipwreck.

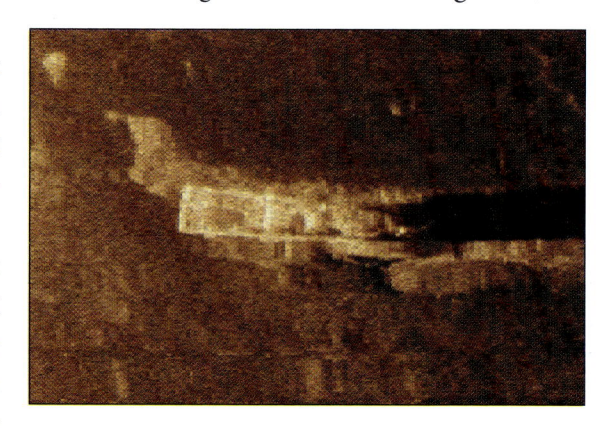

Side-scan sonar image of *CG-56022*.
Image courtesy of Jim Kennard

One of the benefits of announcing a shipwreck discovery is the tendency of new, prized information that comes forward from individuals who have some connection to the life of the boat or its demise. Our discovery of *CG-56022* is certainly a case in point. Some of the secrets we learned after our discovery concerned life aboard the vessel, clarification about her loss, and the details of a secret non-governmental salvage operation.

The Final Chapter of USCG Cable Boat *CG-56022*

CG-56022 underwater. Drawing by Roland E Stevens III

After we announced our discovery, *CG-56022* crewmember Palmer Walker contacted us to tell us his story.

In 1964, the Ninth District Coast Guard acquired a military landing craft (LCM) and then modified it to serve as a cable boat. This cable boat was utilized as a floating platform to repair, remove, install, or renew various submerged cables in all of the Great Lakes. Designated *CG-56022*, the vessel had two screws and was powered by two GM 6-71 diesel engines. The vessel's design included a watertight double bottom and wing tanks on both sides. The lazarette (small store room) and engine room were not watertight as they were fitted with non-watertight ventilation ducts. The cable boat was assigned to USCG Sector Detroit until 1971, when it was re-

Diver and friend of Jim Kennard, Teddy Garlock, diving the USCG-*56022*.

Image courtesy of Teddy Garlock

assigned to USCG Sector Sault Ste. Marie. Movements of the *CG-56022* were directed by work orders issued by the District Engineering Division prior to the start of the season of operation.

Crewmember Palmer Walker describes what life was like aboard *CG-56022*.

> Life on the US Coast Guard (*CG-56022* cable boat), in my opinion, was very relaxed and rewarding. The cable boat was an open-hull landing craft re-fitted to carry large reels of cabling used to repair lighthouse power cables and that was our primary mission. The Corps of Engineers would dredge an area and while doing so, they would often damage the cables to the lighthouses and we would repair them. When repairing cables, we would first locate the power cable on the shore side, lift it, and buoy it off. Then, we would do the same on the lighthouse side. Next, we would determine whether or not to bring the buoys together or splice in a new length of cable. More often, we would end up splicing in a new section. Once the lighthouse was working, we would move on to the next job. There was nothing more beautiful than seeing a functioning lighthouse.

The crew included one Mechanist Mate (MK3) Clancy "Gator" Hull, one Boatswain Mate (BM1) George Perry, and one Seaman/Fireman (SN), that was me. The work season started in mid-March and was supposed to end on November 15, but this date was extended in 1977. We worked hard as most workdays were from dawn to dusk. However, we were able to see many of the hidden gems of the Great Lakes. There were no berths or a mess on the boat so the crew would stay in local hotels. We were paid a TDY (Temporary Duty) for the season. I did not see my family from April until December.

We were very well versed in the normal USCG distress drills such as man-overboard, taking on water, etc. There were survival suits on board and a radio for communications, but there was no life raft. A compass was our only navigational instrument.

Palmer Walker circa 1977.
Image courtesy of Palmer Walker

On May 20, 1977, the Ninth District Coast Guard ordered *CG-56022* to proceed to Holland, Michigan, for cable work upon the completion of hull repairs and an evaluation by the Group Engineer. Material failures further delayed the cable boat departing from Sault Ste. Marie until May 31. From June to October, the cable boat crew was involved in cable replacement and repair in Muskegon, Chicago, Toledo, Sandusky, Lorain, Ashtabula, and Conneaut. Upon completion of the projects in Lakes Michigan and Erie, the next priority was repair work at Oswego. The weather in mid-October was not satisfactory for travel on Lake Ontario from Buffalo to Oswego. So, *CG-56022* made its way to Oswego via the Erie Canal, which took a little more than three days. Shortly after arrival in Oswego the starboard main engine failed and needed to be replaced. The only replacement engine available at that time was one that had been removed from another Coast Guard vessel after it sank off of Mackinaw Island. It was reported that the engine had been surveyed and was considered operational. By November 23, the USCG had replaced the main starboard engine, and upon testing, discovered the maximum limit of its operation was only 1,500 RPM due to vibration. The engine should have been able to produce 2,500 RPM and when the cable boat had a full load on the underperforming engine, it experienced excessive power loss. Further investigation determined that there were a number of other problems with this repurposed engine, which had not been properly surveyed and did not comply with its own specifications. The USCG postponed the work at Oswego but then ordered the crew to complete operations at Fairport, Ohio.

On December 1, *CG-56022* left for Fairport Harbor, Ohio, as ordered. The National Weather Service had issued a gale warning for Lake Ontario later in the day. Palmer Walker recalled:

> There are no ifs, ands, or buts about it. The district wanted us to complete one more job before our trip home. George (Perry) argued that the boat had a three-foot draft and we should have been dry-docked for the winter.[1]
>
> When we left the USCG Station at Oswego, the day started out very good. We had received our weather report and had clear sailing to Rochester, our first port of call. About four to five hours into the trip, George and Gator were sleeping in the cabin behind me and I was at the helm. That was our usual napping area since there was no berthing aboard. A couple of hours later, I noticed the wind was picking up and the whitecaps (waves) were getting larger. I woke up George right away and he could see what was going on. He told me to turn toward the shoreline and to this day, I believe that was the order that saved our lives. As we turned again and started mirroring the shoreline, the waves became more violent. A huge wave came over our gunnel and filled up half of the well. George directed both Gator and I to start the pumps and he took over the helm. Just as the well was empty, another wave crashed upon us and filled the well completely. The pumps were still pumping, however they were making little impact. That's when we moved into survivor mode. We got out of the well and moved towards the helm. Just as we arrived at the helm, another wave crashed into us and tilted the boat downward and the propellers were completely out of the water. We made our distress call and we were able to hear confirmations from as far as Group Detroit. At this point we had no way to reach our survival suits and grabbed onto the stern rail for dear life as the bow began to sink lower in the water. About an hour later, the engines finally

---

[1] With such a shallow draft, a vessel like this would not be stable in big seas, especially knowing that a gale was forecasted.

stopped working and we were able to grab onto the propeller shafts hoping that someone would reach us soon. The boat was bouncing around like an untethered buoy. The day prior to our journey, we had cleared our bilge tanks and the air in them helped to keep us afloat.

By now it was mid-afternoon and the cable boat encountered winds of 15 to 20 knots with 4-foot seas and rain. They were on the edge of the gale that had been predicted for later in the day. When the distress call was made by *CG-56022*, the Coast Guard Cutter *Point Steele* was 18 miles away at Sodus Point, New York.

Palmer Walker remembers:

> Approximately thirty minutes later, I heard engines and when I looked up, a ship's hull was bearing down on us. It was getting dark and I guess they really could not see us. I hollered as loud as I could and the ship started turning away from us. It came around again and lowered its rope ladder. All three of us grabbed on to it and climbed it very quickly. We were placed in the ship's berthing where it was very warm and they wrapped us in blankets surprised that none of us was suffering from hypothermia. Five minutes after we were aboard, the cutter's captain told us that the cable boat had gone down. I'm forever in the other crew's debt.
>
> The USCG cutter *Point Steele* moved us to the USCG Rochester Station. The next day, the District wired us money so that we could get new clothing. Dickies® clothing was authorized at the time, so we went shopping. While we were at the clothing store and at the register waiting to pay, a radio broadcast stated, "Last night three Coast Guardsman were rescued and are now safe in Rochester." The woman at the cash register looks at us and says, "Those poor guys." We thought it was funny. The official US Coast Guard investigation stated that the sinking was by nature and we moved on with our lives.

The discovery of *CG-56022* also led to an unexpected reveal that the boat had actually been discovered by local divers the year after it sank.[2] The USCG apparently abandoned *CG-56022* in May 1979. A group of SCUBA divers from the area wanted to salvage the cable boat. To aid in raising the

---

[2] The *CG-56022* is found at N 43° 17.800' W 77° 19.547'

The USCG cutter *Point Steele*.   Image by the United States Coast Guard

boat to the surface, they sank a huge steel tank 5 feet in diameter and 15 feet long containing rings, ports, and chains next to the stern of the wreck. The bow was already positively buoyant. The tank was then chained to the cable boat. The divers then planned to complete the salvage operation the following weekend. As bad luck happens all too often in salvage operations, during that week a severe storm came up on the lake. The wave action from the storm slammed the tank (which had no air in it) around so bad on the bottom that it became crushed and torn and was made totally useless. One of the divers said that some of the massive chains attached to the cable boat stern lifting rings had snapped. To add to the problem, the boat itself had become damaged and was now sitting in a deeper hole. Subsequent dives revealed that the tank had completely disappeared and was nowhere in the vicinity of the wreck. Storms had probably driven it off. Not long after that, the group fell apart and disbanded. The secret nature of this aborted salvage effort, and the fact that the effort was so short lived, kept this operation a mystery until one of the participants came forward with the details after the discovery.

Palmer Walker left the US Coast Guard in 1981, and retired from the US Army in 2006. He currently works as an Information Technology Specialist at Fort Sam Houston, Texas. He is married to Mechthilde (Maggi) and they have three children; Alicia, Jesse, and Taylor.

Sources:

Mulhall, Tom and Robert Bristol. Private communications.
Times Union [Albany, New York], December 2, 1977.
Walker, Palmer. Personal interview.

(A Version of this chapter was published previously in *Inland Seas®*, Summer 2013 — Volume 69 Page 130 under the authorship of Jim Kennard and Palmer Walker)

60-Fathom Shipwreck:
The Schooner *William Elgin*

In September 1997, Tim Shippee had just completed construction of his home-built side-scan sonar and was anxious to try it out. A local fisherman had recently told Tim about a large bump on the bottom of the lake out from the area of Sandy Pond at the east end of the lake. Tim set up a search grid and headed out on the lake with his 13-year-old daughter, Ariel, to see if they could locate an undiscovered shipwreck. It was a hot day and after several hours of fruitless searching, Tim decided to take a nap and let his daughter drive the boat on the course lines.

Tim with his home-built side-scan used to initially find the William Elgin.   Image courtesy of Tim Shippee

Within 20 minutes, an exciting image appeared on the sonar computer screen. Ariel called to her Dad to come take a look. They had found a shipwreck! Tim and his friend Dennis Gerber later returned to the site and deployed an underwater drop camera in an attempt to video the shipwreck. Unfortunately, this effort failed due to weather and equipment problems. At the time they thought this shipwreck might be the 128-foot steamer *Roberval*, which was lost in a storm in the area in 1916. However, the true identity of this shipwreck was to remain unknown for another nine years.

Ariel Shippee, perhaps the youngest shipwreck discoverer on record.
Image courtesy of Tim Shippee

In 2006, Dan Scoville was looking for a deep shipwreck to test the limits of the ROV that he and a group of students from the

Dan Scoville and Jim Kennard with Dan's first ROV.

Image courtesy of Jim Kennard

Rochester Institute of Technology had just developed. Because we had successfully used the ROV in our identification of the *Milan*, Tim and Dennis invited Dan and me to explore the shipwreck that Tim and Ariel had discovered. What they found was a surprise to everyone.

That summer, Dan, Dennis, and I departed from Oswego. After nearly an hour-long boat ride, we arrived in the area of the unknown shipwreck. After a short while searching, we relocated the wreck, anchored over it, and launched Dan's remote operated vehicle to explore the shipwreck. We deployed the ROV to not only identify what Tim and Ariel had discovered years ago, but to test the depth limits of Dan's design. The ROV descended to the deep lake bottom successfully and gave us an up-close look at the shipwreck. Quagga mussels coat the side of the ship. The ship's anchor is visible. Other equipment, such as a set of chain plates and deadeyes can be seen just beyond the ship's rail. Surprised, but still excited, this was not the steamship that we expected to find. This was not a steamer at all — but a sailing ship!

A second set of chain plates and deadeyes are present as you follow the ship's rail. The ship's holds are in plain sight and to the right is a portion of a circular bracket called a tabernacle that would have secured the mainmast.

Near the stern, the ship's wheel suddenly appears — a beautiful site to see, even if it is encrusted with mussels. Just behind the wheel is the cabin with two windows on either side of the wheel. There is no vessel name on the stern of the ship. Darkness inside the cabin prevents us from discovering its contents. The ship's mainmast hangs out over the port side of the stern. The broken steering mechanism rests on the top of the cabin roof; it may have broken off when the ship hit the lake bottom. Moving now towards the bow, the ship's bilge pump and then the boom cradle are visible. After that, we see the foremast, which is resting on the port side of the deck. The ship's chain locker and winch are still in position.

While exploring this schooner shipwreck, we noticed that there were many suspended particles in the water, watching the video on the monitor felt like we were flying into a snowstorm. This effect was caused by the lights on the ROV being too close to the camera and aimed directly ahead. Our ROV survey proved the wreck was a sailing vessel. Further research and analysis of the ROV survey pointed us toward the schooner *William Elgin* as the possible identity of the wreck.

The hull of the schooner *William Elgin* was built in Oakville, Ontario, in 1853, by shipbuilder M. Simpson and was originally registered as the *Catherine*. During the next 17 years, ownership of the ship changed 10 times. In July 1870, the *Catherine* wrecked on South Bay Point. A year later, she was re-launched by H. B. Rathburn at Mill Point, Ontario, as the

William Elgin. Watercolor by Roland E. Stevens III

schooner *William Elgin*. The *Elgin* measured 99 feet in length with a beam of 23 feet and depth of 10 feet. The ship had a carrying capacity of 12,000 bushels. For the next 17 years, the *Elgin* primarily transported coal from several of the terminals along the southern shore of Lake Ontario to Canadian ports and then returned with lumber or wheat to ports in Lakes Erie and Ontario. Ownership changed four more times during this period.

On Saturday afternoon, May 19, 1888, the *William Elgin left* the New York, Ontario, and Western Railroad Trestle at Oswego with a load of 300 tons of coal consigned to Belleville, Ontario. As the schooner passed Cook Island Dock, she struck bottom and developed a leak. At the time, the crew felt the pumps could handle the leak and under the command of Captain James Savage, she headed out into the lake. About 12 miles off Oswego, it was apparent that the water was coming into the ship too quickly for the pumps to maintain buoyancy. After another few miles, the captain ordered the crew to abandon the sinking vessel. The crew, unfortunately, left all of their personal belongings on the sinking vessel as there was no time to retrieve them. Even the captain suffered personal loss — all of his money went to the bottom with the sinking ship because of the time it took for him to carry the 66-year-old cook to the yawl.

The propeller steamship *Van Allen* passed nearby after the men had taken to their small boat but the crew of the *Van Allen* claimed they hadn't seen the *Elgin's* crew in the yawl. Later, the captain of the *Van Allen* claimed that they had seen the yawl but mistaken it for one of the many small fishing boats that often worked in that area. Fortunately, Captain T. Brokenshire of the schooner *Ocean Wave* had been watching the *Elgin's* progress for some time. When the ship suddenly disappeared, he ordered his crew to keep a sharp lookout for any survivors. The crew of the *Ocean Wave* spotted the survivors and steered a course to rescue the distressed sailors. The *Ocean Wave* dropped the *Elgin's* crew off at Indian Point in Prince Edward County, Ontario; they boarded a steamer for home in Picton. The schooner *William Elgin,* which was worth around $3,000, was not insured and became a total loss.

Over the years, our team has located and identified many shipwrecks based on research and hours of searching the lake bottom. Unidentified discoveries from people like Tim, are another source that has helped our team continue its record of achievement. Thanks Tim, Ariel, and Dennis!

SOURCES:

Oswego Palladium, May 23, 1888.
_____, May 25, 1888.

The Artist and the *Orcadian*

In the fall of 2004, Pultneyville Historical Society invited me to give a presentation on the steamer *Homer Warren* at their annual meeting. Our discovery of the wreck had produced a great deal of press and since the wreck had connections to that community, I was happy to oblige. There was a small group of about 20 active members in attendance that evening. After my talk and the showing of the underwater video of the shipwreck, I answered a few questions from the crowd. Refreshments were served and during that time a couple approached me. The gentleman indicated that on several occasions while sailing on Lake Ontario he had passed over something protruding above the bottom. "Oh boy," I thought, "This is just what Dan and I had hoped to hear from someone attending one of our presentations."

Roland "Chip" Stevens introduced himself and his wife Georgia. Chip has sailed for over 50 years and is an accomplished watercolor artist. Dan and I had been considering adding an artist to our team to illustrate shipwrecks as they rest on the bottom of the lake. Due to the limited visibility in Lake Ontario, our video can only capture small portions of a shipwreck at one time and an artist could put all the pieces together in one image. I offered Chip the opportunity to come out with us the next season to examine the spot where he thought a shipwreck may lay and he accepted. In the spring of 2005, we were all very excited at the prospect

Roland Stevens.   Image courtesy of Roland E. Stevens, III

of finding another shipwreck off Pultneyville. We motored out to the area, deployed the side-scan sonar, and began making a couple of runs around the location where Chip had indicated he had seen something on his depth finder. Nothing was there. We increased our search area but saw only a flat bottom, void of any outcroppings. When using a basic depth finder, it is not unusual to mistake a large number of bait fish hanging close to the bottom for a possible shipwreck. I recall chasing a target many years ago that I thought was a shipwreck but was actually a group of fish that were slowly moving away from the target location. That day on the water we got to know Chip and Georgia and decided to invite them once again to come out for a shipwreck search that we were planning off Sodus Point.

Several weeks later, Dan, Chip, and I returned to the area off Sodus Point where we had found the schooner *Etta Belle* in 2004. This time we deployed the side-scan sonar and sat back to view the image of the lake bottom slowly being printed on a large continuous roll of recording paper. Within two hours, the image of a possible shipwreck appeared. We turned the boat around and headed back to the target location and made several runs to determine the precise spot of the wreck and to obtain more imaging details. Within a few passes we knew it was a sailing ship. I am sure Chip was thinking "WOW! This is really great — just two hours of searching and we discover a shipwreck. How easy is this?" He would soon learn that luck is fickle; she sometimes makes herself known and sometimes disappears for years on end. The next time out and many more after, Chip would spend long days on the lake without finding anything, which is more typical for this kind of exploration.

At the depth where this shipwreck lies there is no visible light to illuminate the ship. We deployed Dan's ROV with onboard cameras and high-intensity lighting to bring back images of the sunken shipwreck. The sailing craft is sitting upright on the bottom. The ship is entirely encrusted with zebra and quagga mussels. There is evidence she sustained a considerable amount of damage as she is broken up, with pieces of the decking either missing or scattered around the wreck site. Much of the forward and mid-deck sections are missing leaving an open area into the hold of the ship, now filled with silt. There is no immediate evidence of cargo. The mainmast and foremast can be seen lying off to the starboard side of the wreck. The bowsprit is visible and the starboard anchor is lying on the bottom next to the bow. The port anchor is resting more than 100 feet away with anchor chain still attached to the ship. The ship's windlass appears to be torn from its mountings on the bow deck. Not much of the cabin area is recognizable, having been torn apart — perhaps from a collision, hitting

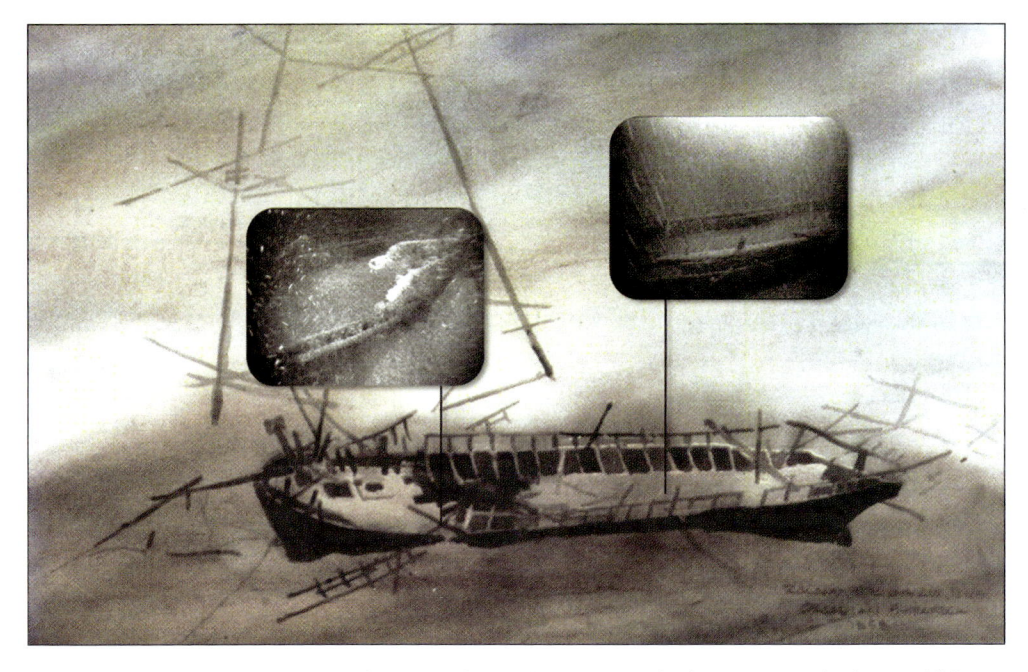

The *Orcadian* on lake bottom. Underwater photos (L-R): portside damage near the bow, midship. Watercolor by Roland E. Stevens III. Updated 2018 images courtesy of Roger Pawlowski

the lake bottom, or blown off by air pressure expelled as the ship sank. The ship's tiller is in its last position on the starboard side of the ship and the attached rudder is still visible at the stern. A few deadeyes and pulley blocks are lying about in the wreckage.

The sailing ship that the three of us located did not have an observable name painted on the stern but other clues helped to identify the vessel. This shipwreck had two masts and a tiller, thus placing the construction of this ship from the 1850s or earlier. After this period, sailing craft utilized a ship's wheel to control the rudder. The extent of the visible damage suggested the possibility of collision. Measurements made by an *Imagenex* sector-scanning sonar[1] mounted on the underwater ROV confirmed the dimensions of the shipwreck as 94 feet in length and a beam of 20 feet. A search through the shipwreck databases provided only one possible candidate that matched the general period of time when the ship was probably built, that had the same measurements, that suffered a collision and sank in the general location where this target was found, the Canadian brigantine

---

[1] Sector-scan sonars are forward-looking imaging sonars utilizing transmitted and reflected underwater sound waves to detect and locate objects or for measuring distance. They are often used to make sure ROVs aren't going to hit something.

Orcadian. The *Orcadian* collided with the *Lucy J. Latham* on May 8, 1858, and sank quickly. Newspapers of the day, like the *Oswego Daily Palladium*, incorrectly printed the name as *Arcadian*, *Arcadia*, or *Acadia*. The Canadian registry of vessels shows the proper name of this ship as *Orcadian*.

In an ideal world, we wish we had seen physical evidence that proved this wreck was brigantine rigged. Brigantine rigged vessels are less common on the Lakes than schooners and would have narrowed the field quite a bit. A brigantine is a two-masted vessel with square sails on the foremast and a fore and aft sail on the mainmast; the mainmast may have upper square sails as well. However, at this wreck site, the mainmast had collapsed and was partially silted over. Worse yet, it may have even been mixed in with the remains of bowsprit, jib boom and top foremast of the *Latham*, which went to the bottom with the *Orcadian* when it sank.

Orcadian was a brigantine rigged sailing ship built at St. Ours, Quebec, in 1854, by C. Richard and owned by Rae & Brothers of Hamilton, Ontario. She had a carrying capacity of 147 tons. On May 8, 1858, she was travelling east to Oswego, New York, when she collided with the schooner *Lucy J. Latham* heading in the opposite direction for the Welland Canal. The *Orcadian* had departed Bayfield, Ontario, on the Canadian shore of Lake Huron, with a cargo of 8,200 bushels of wheat destined for Oswego and consigned to Clark & Gifford of Albany, New York. The *Lucy J. Latham* cleared the port of Oswego early in the evening with a full load of 800 barrels of Onondaga salt bound for Chicago.

At 3 a.m., while performing tacking maneuvers, the *Lucy J. Latham* collided with the side of the *Orcadian*. The accident was reported to have occurred approximately 8 to 10 miles off Big Sodus Bay, near the port of Sodus Point, New York. The *Orcadian* took on a rush of water from the large gap in the side of her hull created by the collision and began to sink immediately. While going down, the mainmast of the *Orcadian* caught on the jib boom of the *Latham*. The bow of the *Lucy J. Latham* was drawn underwater, while her keel at the stern was raised 10 to 12 feet out of the water. For a short period of time, the *Latham* sustained the immense weight of the sinking brigantine until finally it was relieved when her bowsprit, jib-boom, and fore top mast, gave way — all being carried under by the *Orcadian*. Within less than 10 minutes, the *Orcadian* sank in deep water with its cargo of wheat. Captain James Corrigal, his wife, their two children, and the crew took to their yawl boat and were taken safely aboard the *Latham*, which then put about and returned to Oswego.

Roland "Chip" Stevens is a retired architect and working artist whose watercolors are well known in the Rochester area. His paintings have been accepted into numerous national exhibitions. Chip became the third partner in our three-man shipwreck exploration team. His illustrations of our shipwreck discoveries and his knowledge of sailing craft have been a great addition to our team in helping better understand the details of these lost ships.

SOURCES:

Oswego Commercial Advertiser, January 15, 1859, "Great Lakes Losses for 1858".
Oswego Daily Palladium, Monday, May 10, 1858.

Fatal fire on the Steamer *Samuel F. Hodge*

Samuel F. Hodge.
Image courtesy of the Historical Collection of the Great Lakes at Bowling Green State University

The 2007 search season had not been successful and we were losing hope of discovering any new shipwrecks before foul weather arrived. As any shipwreck hunter will tell you, one or two unsuccessful search seasons in a row can lower morale and dampen enthusiasm for spending countless hours on the lake all summer long. We had covered a lot of territory in the western area of Lake Ontario and September, which is known for severe storms, was not far away. Dan and I had good success in the western portions of the lake the two previous seasons, but this year was proving more difficult. All we needed was just one new shipwreck discovery to make all the long days spent in research, preparation, and searching worthwhile. At long last, on August 31, a shipwreck appeared on the side-scan sonar display screen. Clearly, this was not a sailing ship or a barge but some other type of vessel.

Following our standard protocol, we deployed the ROV with onboard cameras and high intensity lighting to bring back images of the discovery.

Samuel F. Hodge on lake Bottom. Underwater photos (L-R): looking toward portside bow, stern deck.   Watercolor by Roland E. Stevens III. Updated 2018 images courtesy of Roger Pawlowski

When we sent the ROV down to explore the shipwreck, we had exceptional visibility. Some natural light from the surface provided enough illumination to allow the low-light cameras to view objects on the shipwreck at a greater distance than with the ROV lights. The shipwreck is upright on the bottom. The frames of the ship protrude high above the remaining hull planking on both sides. Much of the ship's forward and mid decks are covered in silt. Some of the openings to the holds in these areas are just visible. A large steam engine extends above the hull of the ship. At the stern, a single propeller and rudder are almost completely exposed. A closer examination of the timbers shows that this ship had burned. The upper deck and cabins are completely missing as are any masts. During another sonar search later on, we found the masts of the steamer several miles away. The masts had fallen off the ship as it burned and must have drifted towards their final resting place off Oak Orchard.

We identified this target once again by measuring it and testing that data against historical research that matched the location and particulars of the disaster. Measurements made by our sonar equipment and the ROV indicated that the length of the ship was approximately 150 feet and its width was 30 feet. The presence of propeller and steam engine was proof of its propulsion. The ship's final resting place is approximately midway between

Niagara Falls and Rochester, New York. The condition of the burned hull suggested a fire had played some role in the ship's sinking. A search of several shipwreck databases provided only one possible candidate that exactly matched the evidence presented by our discovery, exploration, and examination of the target — the steamer *Samuel F. Hodge*.

Fire at sea is regarded among mariners as the most dangerous hazard to a wooden ship. A small engine fire can quickly spread throughout the entire ship. When a fire grows out of control running from the flames is not an option and assistance to help combat the fire may be many miles and hours away.

The *Hodge*'s propeller.
Updated 2018 image courtesy of Roger Pawlowski

In the early morning hours of July 5, 1896, the steamer *Samuel F. Hodge* was en route from Cleveland, Ohio, to Prescott, Ontario, with a cargo of 600 tons of iron wire. When the ship was off Oak Orchard, New York, a second engineer named O'Connor discovered a fire during his watch. He had orders from the chief engineer not to exceed 80 pounds of steam pressure but he saw the pressure rising above that point. O'Connor hurried to find Martin Deeley, the fireman, to order him to reduce the steam pressure to 80 pounds. As he reached the firehold door, he saw flames coming from around the smokestack. He yelled for Deeley and then ran down to the engine room to start the pumps. However, Deeley was nowhere to be found and had not heard O'Connor. By now the boiler house and after cabin were in flames. The crew was alerted and tried to suppress the fire. When their efforts failed, the crew launched the yawl boats and escaped the burning ship. Two men had to jump overboard to make their escape. One of the owners, H. C. Farrell, was onboard and jumped through a window into the lake. When he was finally picked up, he was suffering from exhaustion. The fire spread so fast that none of the crew was able to get to their belongings. The cook, Paul Jones, wore only his undershirt as he leapt from the burning ship. Thankfully, everyone but Fireman Deeley escaped with their lives.

A brisk wind continued to fan the flames consuming the steamer. The *St. Joseph*, a steamer operating nearby, sighted the burning ship and came to the *Hodge* to offer assistance to her crew. For over an hour the crew of the *St. Joseph* attempted to suppress the fire with water sprayed from the *St. Joseph*'s pumps. But it did little to put out the fire. The intense heat of the fire began to damage the *St. Joseph* so her crew ceased the futile effort. Captain Lewis Elliot, on the *Hodge*, had brought his wife on that trip and commented proudly on her role in helping the crew escape certain death. "My wife had joined me at Buffalo intending to take the trip down the lake to visit our friends in Watertown. It was, therefore, my first care to get her off safely. I ran to my cabin and told her to hurry up … Mrs. Elliot was the bravest member of the first party and directed the men in their rescue of Mr. Farrell and the watchman, Monk." His wife stated, "I did not believe I should be frightened by sudden danger … and was not, even when our lives were in such danger. I supposed my husband would follow me, but he remained on deck and only said, 'You are all right.'"

The *Samuel F. Hodge* was built in Detroit in 1881, and was classed as a steam barge. The ship was owned by the Farrell Brothers of Buffalo, New York, and had an A2 rating.[1] It was valued at $25,000 and insured for $18,000. The cargo was valued at $7,000 and was insured.

Our discovery of the *Hodge* had now charged up our enthusiasm to search for more shipwrecks. For the next month, thanks to a brush of good weather, we continued to survey the western area of Lake Ontario until the foul weather finally arrived and forced us to end the shipwreck search season in early October. We could hardly wait for what we might find next year.

Sources:

British Whig [Kingston, Ontario], July 10, 1896.
Buffalo Evening News, July 6, 1896.
Buffalo Morning Express, July 7, 1896.
Detroit Free Press, July 10, 1896.

---

[1] Underwriters of insurance classified vessels for insurance purposes. An A1 rating was the highest classification, which meant the vessel was believed to be in superior shape.

The Wreck of The *W. Y. Emery*

By John Albright

At one o'clock in the afternoon on Monday, September 25, 1899, the 104-foot, two-masted schooner, *W. Y. Emery*, cleared the Port of Charlotte near Rochester, New York, with a crew of four men under the command of Captain William Mitchell. The ship was bound for its homeport of Kingston, Ontario, with a cargo of 400 tons of bituminous coal. Although the weather on the lake was squally, Captain Mitchell had no special concerns as such weather was to be expected on the lake in September. However, things soon changed.

At ten o'clock that evening, one of the most violent gales of that year struck the *Emery* from the northwest. She was then about 50 miles out from Charlotte, in the open waters of Lake Ontario. Captain Mitchell brought her about to ease the pounding she was taking, but to no avail. The 32-year-old wooden vessel, with its heavy cargo, could not take the strain and her seams opened up. She began taking on water.

Upon discovering the water below, the crew took to the pumps and fought the gale and the rising water throughout the night. By morning, the *Emery* was about two miles off the town of Ontario, New York and in serious trouble. She had been stripped of her sails by the wind and was still taking on water. She deployed both her heavy anchors and raised distress flags.

Fortunately, observers on shore spotted the vessel's distress signal and went to town and telegraphed the lifesaving station at Charlotte. Captain Gray of the lifesaving station immediately chartered the steam tug *Proctor* and set out with his lifesaving crew with surfboat in tow. Upon arriving at the stricken vessel, the lifesavers had great difficulty getting Captain Mitchell and his crew off the vessel. The last crewman was removed just as the water closed over the *Emery*'s decks and she sank to the bottom. The captain was able to rescue some articles of value from his cabin, including considerable money and his clearance papers.

The tug returned to Charlotte, arriving there about 4:15 p.m. with the captain and crew of the *W. Y. Emery* saved. According to the 1900 Annual Report of the United States Life Saving Service, "The rescued men were given dry clothes from the stores of the Women's National Relief Association. The master was injured by being struck by the main boom, and the keeper had a physician summoned to sew up a gash in his face. The men remained at the station two days."

In 2000, Rec Divers, Inc., a Rochester-area SCUBA diving club, launched a search for the *W. Y. Emery*. With the help of significant research by the Ontario Town Historian, Liz Albright, and valuable information from area residents, a search was initiated. The search itself, and diving operations, were organized by myself, owner and captain of the *Half Moon*. The first two years of the search involved systematically covering two square miles of the lake bottom with a "fish finder" which picked up unusual structures on the bottom. Spot dives were made on any promising "bump" which could have been the *Emery*. Unfortunately, the lake bottom is strewn with hundreds of large rocks and rock piles. As a result, the search lasted seven years.

Once the search grid had been covered with the fish finder and spot dives, the more labor intensive process of "eye-balling" the bottom was begun. This was done by using a sweep line to swim circles around the search boat's anchor in an overlapping grid pattern. It is worth noting that the search method employed was probably the only practical method of finding this wreck given the rugged contour of the bottom and the numerous large rocks and rock piles that would have hidden the wreck from side-scan sonar. Furthermore, it is more fun to dive!

Finally, on September 8, 2007, after hundreds of dives by members of the search team, the remains of the *Emery* were located. On that day, Susan Burke and Russ Palum were in the water swimming the usual circle pattern while I remained onboard enjoying a cup of coffee. Suddenly, Susan surfaced and began screaming. Fearing the worst, I dropped my coffee and prepared to go to her aid. Seconds later, Russ surfaced to announce "We found it!"

The hull was broken apart undoubtedly from the impact with the rock bottom, the weight of the coal, and possibly from the force of later storms. The wheel was standing upright and the anchors were in a line consistent with the maritime practice for ships of that era in a storm. Artifacts were scattered around the rock bottom and many were encrusted with zebra mussels. The most exciting find was the compass, which was intact and still pointed north! Among

Wheel from the *W. Y. Emery*.   Image courtesy of Alan Klauda

Anchor from the *W.Y. Emery*. Image courtesy of Alan Klauda

Compass from the *W.Y. Emery*. Image courtesy of Russ Palum

other artifacts found were tools that would have been used by the crew, galley items like pieces of crockery, and the iron stove, which was flattened. The *Emery* is the only ship known to have wrecked off Ontario, New York, and the eventual discovery of coal, her cargo that fateful day, provides strong evidence as to her accurate identification.

The wreck was immediately registered with the State of New York and in 2008, the Club was granted permission to retrieve some artifacts under the supervision of Dr. LouAnn Wurst, Professor of Archeology at SUNY Brockport. Artifacts were brought to the surface, carefully photographed and catalogued and sent to Brockport for processing prior to being placed at Heritage Square Museum in Ontario, New York, where the display will remain on loan from the New York State Museum.

Over the seven-year search, many other members of the Club participated including Ray Scheffler, Tom Lombard, Eric Happ, Alan Klauda, Mike Culver, Mark and Sandy Bohner, John Brooks and Norm Meaker.

SOURCES:

Arcadian Weekly Gazette [Newark, New York], September 27, 1899.
Daily Palladium [Oswego, New York], September 27, 1899.
Democrat & Chronicle [Rochester, New York], September 27, 1899.
Record [Sodus, New York], September 29, 1899.
Rochester Herald, September 27, 1899.
Union and Advertiser [Rochester, New York], September 27, 1899.
United States. Treasury Department. Office of Life-Saving Service. *The Annual Report of the United States Life-Saving Service for the fiscal year ending June 30, 1900*. Washington: Government Printing Office, 1901.

Living on his family's farm on the shore of Lake Ontario, **John Albright** grew up listening to stories about the history of the lake and tales of lost ships. As a teenager, he joined Sea Explorers Ship 110 and learned nautical skills and seamanship and was also introduced to scuba diving. He has spent most of his life around the water and boats. He has earned his Coast Guard Captains license; and as a practicing attorney, he has worked with BOAT US investigating boating accidents and representing their members. Now retired, John continues to dive and wreck hunt with Rec Divers, Inc., a local dive club.

THE *ONTARIO*
2008

The British Warship *Ontario*

HMS *Ontario*. Watercolor by Roland E. Stevens III

For decades, His Majesty's Ship (HMS) *Ontario* was considered one of the few "Holy Grail" shipwrecks in the Great Lakes. Many a diver and shipwreck hunter had searched Lake Ontario without success. The desire to find her was fueled in part by the publication of shipwreck books in the 1960s that speculated that a British payroll might be onboard.[1] Not surprisingly, as each decade passed, these authors inflated the value of the treasure.

---

[1] This was far from the actual truth, as any payroll for the troops would have come from Carleton Island, and the *Ontario* started that fateful night from Fort Niagara. Also there has never been any mention of a payroll in the British documented reports.

Never let it be said that an author might let a good fact get in the way of the sale of his own book![2] In the 1970s, I was not immune to treasure fever.[3] One summer, fellow divers Ralph Sylvester, Paul Grabowski, and I headed out to the Golden Hill State Park, about 50 miles west of Rochester, to find those treasures aboard *Ontario*. It was not quite as easy as we had thought. In those early years, it was very difficult to run an effective search grid more than half a mile or so from shore. LORAN-C positioning was not practically available on Lake Ontario until 1980; the GPS navigation system came about later in the 1990s. As I began doing my own research, it became apparent to me that the *Ontario* foundered much farther from shore and it could be anywhere in an area as vast as 600 square miles. The depths off the southern shore of western Lake Ontario can quickly reach nearly 600 feet. Even if we could find this shipwreck, I would not be able to dive on it safely due to its depth. After a few years of futile searching, I decided to give up. The admiralty drawing of HMS *Ontario* hung on my office wall for another 34 years as a reminder of this very elusive shipwreck.

The *Ontario*'s loss and the subsequent search effort by the British are documented in the *Haldimand Papers* covering a period from 1758 through

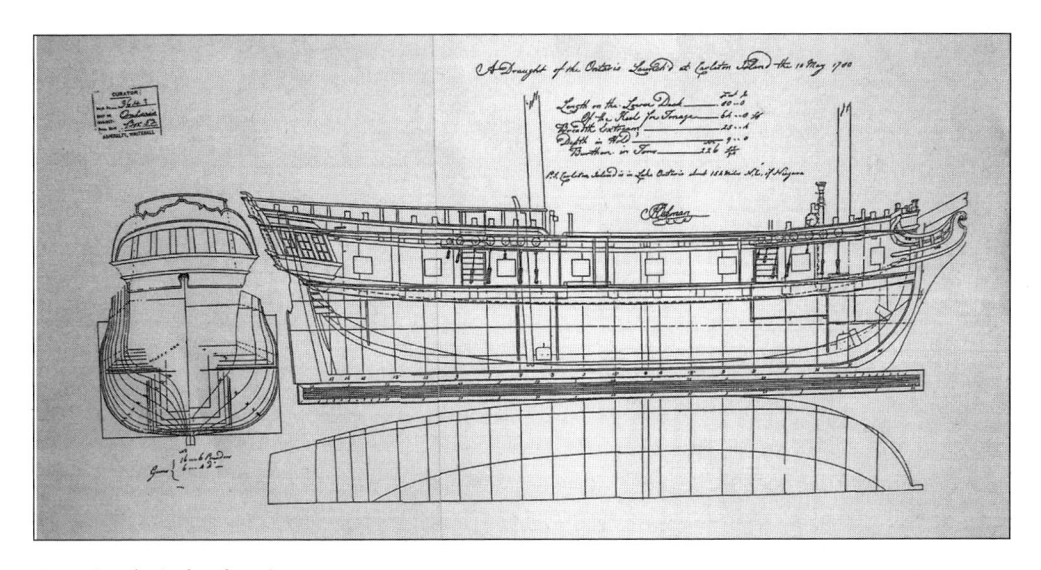

Ontario admiralty drawing.

---

[2] One author that portrays the *Ontario*'s history with accuracy and skill is Arthur Britton Smith. Smith's book, *Legend of the Lake*, does not chase tales of treasure but instead is an excellent treatise on the *Ontario* in the context of the conflict between the British and the Americans.

[3] Over the next three decades, the shipwrecks I discovered helped me to appreciate the historical value of these underwater archaeological sites.

1784 on 115 rolls of microfilm. The *Haldimand Papers* are the written correspondence of Frederick Haldimand, and cover his time as commander and governor in what is now Canada during the French and Indian War as well as the Revolutionary War. Our Canadian friend, Guy Morin, assisted in the research of the *Ontario*. He scrolled through the reports of the *Ontario's* demise as recorded in the *Haldimand Papers,* which are stored in the National Archives of Canada located in Ottawa. I reviewed those specific documents again for any clues that might help us narrow our search effort, but found little concrete information. Why restart the search for the *Ontario* without new information to narrow that huge search area? When we proved that we could effectively explore a deep-water wreck with Dan's ROV, the size of the search area paled in comparison to our enthusiasm to see this wreck up-close. Large search areas can be overcome by time and patience, particularly if the reward is exploring what would be the oldest discovered shipwreck on the Great Lakes. In 2008, Dan, Chip, and I returned to the waters of western Lake Ontario to find the wreck that had eluded me for over three decades.

Towards the end of May, we came upon a target near the very edge of the side-scan sonar's range of 660 feet. At that distance, we could not determine what the target was, but we were confident that we had found a shipwreck and the first one of the season. Making a turn with the sonar with nearly four tenths of a mile of cable takes a long time and requires very careful maneuvering so as not to run the sonar sensor towfish into the lake bottom. We carefully made the turn and on this pass, we were within 100 feet of the new shipwreck. It was difficult to see much of the deck as the side of the target was blocking the deck view from the sonar. Yet, we were able to see two very long masts with at least one fighting top. This looked very promising. We decided to try to make another pass by the ship to see if we could get a more defined image of the deck. Unfortunately, my calculations were off and what followed left us gasping for breath. As the sonar towfish made its pass, my calculations put the towfish right between each mast! It was like being in a car wreck, when all you can do is hang on and pray. Fortunately, the towfish and cable made it between the masts without being caught or damaged. Due to the target's depth, had the towfish gotten snagged, it would have been game over for the sonar equipment and the season! Not to mention the mast might have snapped and caused damage to the shipwreck due to the pressure. The return sonar image was worth the miscalculated pass as it showed both masts were over 80 feet in length, each with a fighting top extant. It also confirmed that the target was leaning to port by 45 degrees. Examining the image, it was as if we were involved in a

The British Warship *Ontario*

Ontario underwater.   Watercolor by Roland E. Stevens III

baseball game and our pitcher had a perfect game going into the seventh inning — nothing was said, but all three of us were thinking this might be the *Ontario*.

We found this shipwreck between Niagara Falls and Rochester, New York, in an area of the lake where the depth extends to more than 500 feet. I am sure each of us wished he could dive and explore this wreck in person, even if only for a few minutes. However, due to depth limitations, we knew that we would have to once again deploy Dan's ROV to confirm the identity of the shipwreck. But it would be two more weeks before the lake was calm enough to do so. Those were two weeks of constant anticipation!

We arrived at the shipwreck in the middle of the night when the lake conditions were perfect for our exploration. We dropped anchor near the target hoping that its weight would be sufficient to hold our boat in place. Dan deployed his remote operated vehicle with its onboard cameras and high-intensity lighting to bring back video images of the discovery. What we saw topside from the ROV can only be described as the fulfillment of a life's dream. First, lying next to the starboard side of the stern is a longboat. The ship's big rudder stands at the stern, and just above it, there are seven windows. The rudder is hard to starboard. When I saw the windows, I was convinced we had found the *Ontario,* as this matched perfectly with the

Ontario from above. Watercolor by Roland E. Stevens III

ship's admiralty drawings I had seen when researching the vessel and looked at every day on my office wall. As we explored the ship with the ROV, Dan, Chip, and I watched in reverent silence as we thought about all the men, women, and children who died on that fateful night at the end of October 1780. To this day it continues to be the largest loss of life in a maritime disaster on Lake Ontario.

Above the stern windows, the flagstaff up to the knob, stands proudly. We easily imagined the Union Jack waving in the breeze. Quarter galleries are located on either side of the stern area of the *Ontario*. A quarter gallery is a kind of enclosed balcony with windows that are typically placed on the sides of the stern-castle, a high tower-like structure at the back of a ship that housed the officers' quarters. Both quarter galleries are still present with some of the window glass still in place. Dan directed the ROV to the starboard side of the ship. There, all of the gun ports are closed and coated with several layers of quagga mussels. Many of the deadeyes and belaying pins that were used to secure lines are still located on the rails of the ship. Around mid-ship, boarding steps, built into the ship's starboard side, are undisturbed.

As one moves toward the bow, spars lay across the deck of the ship, perhaps fallen away from the foremast. At the bow is the ship's headrail that provided protection for the hull where an anchor hung. Two of the large anchors are clearly visible. One anchor is still secure in its original position on the port side and the other sits off to the starboard side of the shipwreck. A portion of the bowsprit remains and just below it is a beautifully carved stem scroll. Also at the bow, the two, six-pounder bow chaser cannons lay on their sides having come loose from their original positions when the ship went over on its side. Moving aft towards the foremast and peeking out from behind it is the ship's belfry. The bell is still in place ready to ring out commands for the crew. The bell is a real jewel and is a beautiful sight to see. All of the companionway and waist covers are gone leaving a slight opening to the deck below. To this day, this area remains unexplored as silt prevents us from taking the ROV into the interior of the *Ontario*.

The masts rise up over 80 feet from the deck. We documented both masts in their entirety and near the top were given the opportunity through the ROV to "sit" in the fighting top as if we were on watch for rebel colonial forces. The foremast is missing the top gallant, but the one on the mainmast is still intact. Along the middle of the port side are the broken remains of one of the small boats that the *Ontario* carried on its deck. Next to the mainmast are two bilge pumps and the booby hatch that leads down to the officer's quarters. While still afloat, the ship's binnacle would have been found in this area. It was found among the wreckage on shore. Next, the tiller arm sits as it was pushed all the way over to the port side of the ship. Under the middle of the tiller rests a small four-pounder deck cannon. A larger six-pounder cannon, probably the starboard chaser, lies near the end of the tiller. While in operating condition, both cannons would have been mounted on the stern deck of the ship. They appear to have broken free and landed on the tiller with a weight estimated at approximately 2,000 pounds. Perhaps this event forced the *Ontario* hard over to port preventing the ship from recovering and ultimately leading her to founder. Next to the tiller, the port stern chaser cannon sits tipped over onto its side.

Every time I examine the underwater footage of the HMS *Ontario*, I am in awe. All of our discoveries up to this point are historically important, but locating and identifying the HMS *Ontario* is certainly at the top. Not only did we find the oldest to be discovered shipwreck on the Great Lakes, but we opened up the world to this remarkable story that, unfortunately, is rarely covered in textbooks on the American Revolution.

During the Revolutionary War (1775–1783) the British controlled Lake Ontario to insure that the lucrative fur trade remained uninterrupted.

Located at the west end of Lake Ontario stood the British outpost Fort Niagara and at the east end of the lake, only a few miles down the Saint Lawrence River on Carleton Island, was Fort Haldimand. In July 1778, the British Commander-in-Chief Frederick Haldimand ordered the establishment of a shipyard on the North Bay of Carleton Island. The task of building a new warship was given to Master Shipwright John Coleman. Coleman trained in his craft at the Royal Navy dockyards in England and prior to receiving his orders to move to Fort Haldimand, Coleman had been involved in repairs to two British vessels at Fort Niagara. In the fall of 1779, construction of a new warship began at the Carleton Island Shipyard. The armed snow[4] was completed on May 10, 1780, and christened *Ontario*. The ship measured 80 feet in length from bow to stern with a burden weight or cargo capacity of 226 tons. She had a beam of 25 feet and a depth of 9 feet. The *Ontario* was built with two large masts rising nearly 80 feet above the flat deck. Behind the mainmast was a smaller "snow mast" which allowed a separate gaff-rigged sail to be hoisted avoiding entanglement with the spars on the mainmast. Two, six-pounder bow chaser cannons were positioned at the front of the boat and two stern chaser cannons were located in the rear. Additional four-pounder cannons could be positioned on the main deck as needed. Below on the gun deck were locations for 14 or more six-pounder cannons. The officers' quarters, fashioned by moveable partitions, were found near the stern on the gun deck; seamen slept in hammocks mid-ship. Below the gun deck was the hold containing storerooms, the powder magazine, shot locker, and some limited space for additional passengers.

From May through October 1780, the *Ontario* transported troops, stores, and civilian merchandise across Lake Ontario, stopping at Niagara, Carleton Island, and Oswego. During this period, the *Ontario* never came under attack from American forces. In late September 1780, the *Ontario* sailed from Carleton Island to Fort Niagara fully loaded with troops, Mohawk, Seneca, and Onondaga scouts, canoes, and supplies. The return trip a month later would be its last and fatal voyage.

In the early afternoon of All Hallow's Eve 1780, the British warship HMS *Ontario* departed Fort Niagara on a two-day journey across Lake Ontario to Fort Haldimand. The *Ontario*'s unofficial personnel count of 120 passengers consisted of crew, military personnel, several women and children, members of the First Nations, and possibly American prisoners of

---

[4] Snow refers to a method of rigging. It consists of two masts with square sails and a third mast placed directly behind the main mast that holds a lateen, or gaff, rigged sail.

war. The *Ontario* was commanded by Captain James Andrews, a seasoned naval officer and the commodore of the Lake Ontario squadron. When the voyage began, there was a fresh wind coming out of the southwest which should have made for perfect conditions for an eastward trip. Weather conditions can change quickly on Lake Ontario and unfortunately for those aboard the *Ontario* conditions changed dramatically on that day. Around 8 p.m. that evening, the winds died down and then abruptly altered direction coming now from the northeast and blowing at gale force. Those on the deck of the *Ontario* must have worked frantically to take down some of the sails in an effort to turn the ship around and head back to Fort Niagara. Very soon the high winds and waves would have caused the *Ontario* to roll back and forth violently. Since no member of the crew or passengers survived, it is impossible to know exactly what happened that tragic evening. From the wreck site, we documented that two of the cannons in the stern of the ship along with their carriages broke free from their positions, rolled across the deck and landed against the tiller arm. We think this happened during the storm and that this event must have forced the ship hard over to port. No recovery would have been possible with over 2,000 pounds of cannon and carriages ramming the tiller. The *Ontario* went over on its port side catapulting those on deck into the water and trapping all those below as the lake water cascaded into the ship through the open companionways and waist passage, an open area between the masts that allowed smoke from cannon fire to escape.

The day after the *Ontario* foundered, a group of British Rangers led by Colonel John Butler was returning from Oswego along the south shore of Lake Ontario. They came upon several of the *Ontario*'s small launch boats, hatchway gratings, binnacle, compasses, blankets, and several hats that had drifted ashore in the area that is known today as Golden Hill State Park. The park is located 30 miles east of Fort Niagara in New York. One of the hats was identified as belonging to Captain James Andrews. Following the reported loss of the *Ontario*, the British conducted a wide search on the lake and over 55 miles of shoreline. A few days later, only the ship's sails were seen adrift in the lake. In late July 1781, six bodies from the *Ontario* were found approximately 12 miles east of the Niagara River near Wilson, New York. After more than eight months in the water and exposure on shore, the identity of the individuals could not be established. They were buried on land near where they were found and a cairn was placed over the gravesite. This was the extent of items from the *Ontario* found by the British.

The table below is the official British account of those who perished on the Ontario.

	Officers	Conductors	Sergeants	Corporal	Drummers	Privates	Total
Navy	2	—	—	—	—	29	31
Royal Artillery	1	1	—	—	—	1	3
Kings 84th Rgt.	1	—	—	—	—	3	4
Kings 34th Rgt	1	—	2	1	1	30*	35
Rangers	—	—	—	—	—	2	2
Passengers	—	—	—	—	—	1	1
Indians	—	—	—	—	—	4	4
TOTAL	5	1	2	1	1	70	80

*including 4 women and 5 children

Note: There were no prisoners-of-war officially listed by the British, however private correspondence by an individual living at Fort Niagara indicated that there may have been up to 120 people on board the ship including 30 American prisoners.[5]

The *Ontario* is the oldest shipwreck ever discovered in the Great Lakes and is probably the oldest fully intact British warship in the world. The ship is in such good condition that one can imagine raising it to sail again. Our exploration to identify the target as the HMS *Ontario* created over 80 minutes of video imagery. For a shipwreck enthusiast like me, spending time on a wreck like the *Ontario* is priceless. Our video documentation of the wreck is so extensive there is no need to return to the site. Furthermore, HMS *Ontario* is the property of the British Admiralty, as nations do not abandon their warships. The shipwreck site of the *Ontario* is considered a war grave at the request of the British government.

SOURCES:

Haldimand, Frederick. Haldimand Papers (1758–1784). Library and Archives Canada.

Smith, Arthur Britton. *Legend of the Lake: The 22-Gun Brig Sloop* Ontario *1780*. New Discovery Edition. Kingston: Quarry Press, 2009.

---

[5] Letter, Francis Goring to Jas. Crespel, August 1, 1781 (Smith, p. 140)

Weather Behind the Sinking of HMS *Ontario*

By Robert Hamilton

Over the years, there have been several theories put forth as to the weather related cause for the foundering of HMS *Ontario*. In order to investigate this issue without introducing speculation, it is necessary to reconstruct the known meteorological conditions in the region. Since organized weather observations were not taken during the 18th century, this is a challenging task. Historic information had to be mined through archival research of ship logs, personal diaries, journals and letters from frontier forts, and finally from limited newspaper accounts.

Up to this point, popular theories about the foundering of the *Ontario* placed the blame squarely on the shoulders of the Great Hurricane of 1780 or on the presence of a strong nor'easter. Interestingly, while research was able to confirm the presence of both storm systems, it was also conclusive in ruling out both as the underlying culprit.

The Great Hurricane

There are many archived accounts of the Great Hurricane of 1780, including that from the *New Jersey Gazette* and the *Pennsylvania Packet*, both colonial newspapers based in Philadelphia. The following excerpt from the *Packet* details the devastation produced from the storm. "…at Barbados, the greater part of the town blown down, upwards of three thousand persons perished. Not one vessel saved except some that got to sea and a great part of the island washed away. In Grenada, much damage done to the states, not one vessel saved except some that got to sea. At St Vincent, a transport with 300 soldiers, two souls only saved; a frigate of 36 guns, three hundred and forty men, one man saved."

This Category 5 hurricane with winds in excess of 200 mph, also known as the Hurricane San Calixto II, is one of the strongest and most destructive on record for the tropical Atlantic. In all, it was responsible for the deaths of over 27,000 people. It completely destroyed the British fleet at St. Lucia and made the French fleet suffer an even greater loss in number of ships. In fact, this hurricane killed more British soldiers than the entire Revolutionary War, so it played an important, and often ignored, role in turning the tide of the war itself. Despite these horrific details, it did not play a role in the foundering of the HMS *Ontario*.

Popular speculation suggests that the hurricane tracked up the east coast of the United States to Nova Scotia before sharply turning southwest to follow the St Lawrence River to Lake Ontario. Given hurricane climatology from 1851 to present and an understanding of autumn jet stream patterns over North America, this track is extremely unlikely — if not climatologically implausible. Supporting this analysis are two historical accounts.

The first account comes from the diary of Elizabeth Drinker, a socialite in Philadelphia. Like most personal journals, the majority of her entries pertained to day-to-day experiences, but she also had a habit of noting significant weather. If the hurricane did indeed follow the speculated track, it would probably be close enough to generate conspicuous or unusual weather in her area. During the time frame that the hurricane was theorized to be passing New Jersey, her only weather related entry was "…went away this afternoon. I went to see SW who I hope continues to mend. *Very fine weather.*"

Meanwhile on the St. Lawrence River, the British merchant ship, the *Fame*, was anchored near Quebec. The ship's log noted a "southwest breeze" on October 30, that was followed by a "clear night." On the day that the HMS *Ontario* foundered (October 31), the *Fame* had the following written its log: "At 6 this morning, weighed from under Crane Island with a fresh breeze at SW. The greatest part of our fleet following us, at 9 almost calm. At ½ past 10 anchored in 5 fathoms abreast of the Tower and of Goose Islands, light rain from the ENE at 2 PM, have our anchor up". The following day, November 1, the log continued, "Fore part of this day strong gales at ENE and cold frosty weather at noon."

These entries are by no means a description of a passing hurricane or even a weakened tropical system. The weather should have been balmy or at least unseasonably mild, but it was noted several times that it was chilly or frosty. As for the wind references, it is crucial to note that the mention of a "fresh breeze" or "strong gales" has no basis to any standardized wind speed measurements up to that point in history. While it would be easy to equate the wind descriptions to those used from the Beaufort wind scale, this would be impossible since the scale was not developed until more than 30 years later and was not made a standard for ship logs on Royal Navy vessels until the late 1830s and for non-Naval use until the 1850s. In other words, the descriptions of the wind were totally subjective to its author.

Another excellent source of information that can be used to dispute the hurricane theory are two letters that were sent to General Frederick Haldimand, the acting British Commander-in-Chief and Governor of the Province of Quebec (essentially Governor of Canada). These letters were sent by the commanding officers at Niagara and Fort Halidmand to inform the British military hierarchy of the foundering of the *Ontario*.

In a letter from Brigadier General Watson Powell, Commanding at Niagara, to General Haldimand, "We are under great Apprehensions for the *Ontario*, which sailed from Hence on the 31st October with Colonel Bolton, Lieut. Royce and 25 of the 34th Regiment. A violent gale came on that evening about eight o'clock, and from several of her gratings, oars, part of her Quarter Gallery, Binnacle and other things being found upon the beach the next day by the troops returning from Oswego, there is no doubt that she must have suffered considerable damage, even if she is not lost. I have since sent the *Mohawk* to ask along the shore, but nothing more has been found, she must therefore have foundered." The letter does not mention heavy rain or even unsettled weather during the following days when a search was made of the south shore of the lake.

The same conclusion can be made from the letter sent from Alex'r Fraser, Commandant, Fort Haldimand. "She sailed on the 31st in the afternoon. A most violent storm came on the same evening from the Northeast, wherein she is supposed to have overset or foundered near a place called Golden Hill, about thirty miles from Niagara, as her boats, the gratings of her hatchway, the binnacle, compasses, and glasses…were picked up along the shore by Col. Butler on his way from Oswego to Niagara. This account is brought by the *Mohawk*, which is just arrived from above having searched all the south shore of the lake without having any other discovery of the *Ontario*." Again, there is no description of a prolonged storm, which is what you would expect from a large tropical system. Additionally, one could easily infer from the phrasing, "a most violent storm came on the same evening," that the storm was sudden and relatively short lived. In fact, visual examination of the wreck strongly supported that this was a sudden, and likely surprising, event. Such would not be the case with a large storm system, but more typical of a smaller scale weather event such as a thunderstorm or line of storms.

THE NOR'EASTER

Numerous sources of weather information conclusively support that indeed, a strong, dynamic storm system did exist along the Northeast coast around the time of the foundering of the *Ontario*. It would therefore be easy for someone to tie the two events together, especially if they did not have access to historic local weather observations and were not trained in synoptic meteorology.[1] Unfortunately, a detailed inspection of the previously unknown facts revealed a serious flaw in the theory that this particular

---

[1] Synoptic meteorology has traditionally been concerned with the analysis and prediction of large-scale weather systems, such as extratropical cyclones and their associated fronts and jet streams.

storm played a role in the demise of the British frigate. The timelines simply do not match up.

William Adair, a colonist in Lewes, Delaware, kept a detailed weather notebook that included daily entries for sky cover, wind direction, atmospheric pressure, temperatures, and significant weather. These observations would prove very valuable, especially given that his location is a prime area where nor'easters become organized and often experience significant strengthening. During the last two days of October 1780, his log indicated that the air pressure had dropped from 1014 mb to nearly 1000 mb, while winds veered from the north to the southeast. This was followed by a "snowstorm" on November 1 that took place while winds shifted from the north to the northwest and the air pressure rebounded to nearly 1014 mb. Clear chilly conditions were then noted for Nov 2 with a continued rise in air pressure. This series of observations accurately describe what could be experienced if a storm had developed in the vicinity of the Delmarva Peninsula. While it is not possible to gauge the intensity of the storm from these observations alone (since the intensifying storm was likely well off the coast), the fact that it was strong enough to generate a snowstorm in this part of the country at the start of November suggests that the storm was quite unusual — and likely quite strong.

Climatology using data since 1950 reveals how unusual a snowstorm is for the Delmarva Peninsula for the month of November. There have only been three storms that produced a minimum of four inches of snow and only a pair that have generated at least 10 inches of accumulation for that region during the past 65 years — and that is considering the **entire** month of November. Logically, these numbers would be even lower for an event that **only** includes the first day or two. The mere fact that William Adair mentions a "snowstorm" to start the month is significant in its own right. It would require a highly anomalous storm system to support accumulating snow at this time.

While the unusual nature and intensity of this storm would be very favorable for supporting an argument of what caused the sinking of the *Ontario*, the data suggests that the storm did not intensify along the coast until the day AFTER the foundering. Being some 400 miles from central Lake Ontario, it is also unlikely that a still developing (immature) storm would be able to generate impactful gale force winds from that distance. Even if such winds were possible, they would increase over a period of hours and not suddenly strike a region as described in the letters to General Haldimand.

A little more than a hundred miles to the north, near Lancaster, Pennsylvania, the colonial army had in its possession a small group of British prisoners of war. Since there were no prison camps, these unfortunate soldiers traveled with their captors. One of these prisoners was a British ensign named Thomas Hughes. To help pass the time, Hughes kept a journal of his travels with the colonial army. On October 31 he noted, "Thunder, lightning and hail storm — followed by a deep snow." This entry gives credence to the information gleaned about a snowstorm from the William Adair weather journal, which corresponds to the presence of a significant storm off the coast. Interestingly, the weather description offered by Hughes is eerily similar to what is observed with early season lake-effect snowstorms and many coastal snowstorms. These particular weather events contain an environment that is very conducive for electrification within the clouds. "Warmer" air from the underlying body of water and the adjacent air mass encourages a deeper, mixed phase of various hydrometers needed for a charge to develop. Given a deep enough cloud, these charges can then separate so that lightning can be generated. During these electrified events, graupel, which is partially melted snow, is often mistaken for hail. Graupel is an essential ingredient for charges to develop within the turbulent cloud, so its presence during or immediately before a snowstorm is often accompanied by thunder and lightning.

Meanwhile further north off Long Island, New York, a portion of the British fleet was lying in wait for the French to appear. The same storm that dumped snow on the Mid Atlantic region apparently played a major role in this pending naval battle. From the logbook of the British brig, *Royal Oaks*, it was noted that clear skies and light breezes from the WNW were experienced on October 31. Conditions quickly deteriorated the following day, as "strong" northerly gales with rain developed during the morning hour. This was followed by "fresh gales" in the afternoon and evening that were accompanied by snow and rain. The entries for the ensuing couple of days continued to describe "strong gales from the north-northeast that gradually backed to the northwest. These daily remarks accurately describe a storm system that would have been stalled — or moving very slowly to the north along the coast.

In a letter penned by Admiral Mariot Arbuthnot to Commodore Sir Peter Parker, additional details were given about the actions of the British fleet just prior to and during the involvement with the coastal storm. "I had the honor to inform you in my letter of the 29th that I had appeared and anchored off Rhode Island with His Majesties Ships under my command equal in point of force to the enemy under De Ternay. I remained there until the 2nd in expectation that some move on their part might enable me to act with effect but no consideration of national or personal motives could prevail on them to risqué an action.

"On that day a gale of wind at NE obliged me to seek refuge in Gardiners Bay or to be blown off the shore. I chose the former and a few hours placed me here in safety from the elements. The gale continued with violence for three days and on the first interval of fair weather I detached the *Adament* off the Port of Rhode Island to reconnoiter the enemy; but scarce had they put to sea when the wind blew from the same point with increasing strength."

While this historical information continues to support the presence of a strong storm along the coast, the detailed timeline from the ship's logbook and subsequent letter also confirm that the storm could not have been involved with the foundering of the *Ontario*.

GREAT LAKES STORM

All of the weather information up to this point pertained to what was happening between Lake Ontario and the East Coast. The final pieces of information came from the west, where the British brig, the *Welcome*, was anchored in Detroit. It was obvious from the entries in the ship's log that some sort of organized weather system pushed through that area in the days leading up to, and including, October 31.

On Saturday, October 28, it was noted that there was a fresh breeze from the east. This was followed by fresh northwest gales and a little rain the following day. On the day before the *Ontario* went down, the *Welcome* recorded WSW winds and "squally weather." While the weather was uneventful as the HMS *Ontario* sailed east from Fort Niagara on October 31, fresh northwest gales "with a dab of snow and hail" were reported back in Detroit. Finally on November 1, a fresh WNW breeze with frosty weather was recorded, along with afternoon winds that were blowing too hard to allow for the crew of the *Welcome* to load.

The fact that the crew of the *Welcome* described unsettled conditions for a stretch of several days, suggested that a slow-moving, or stalled, weather system was in the vicinity. While this type of weather system would not be conducive for sudden changes in wind speed or direction, it would accurately fit the model of a Great Lakes storm.

Research of more than 140 years of weather records, revealed the presence of at least 150 "Great Lakes" storms (minimum pressure 1010mb) during a 15-day period based around the October 31 foundering of the *Ontario*. Despite this climatological wealth of storms during this calendar window, not one scenario could be found where a Great Lakes low would produce **sudden** northeast gales on Lake Ontario. As in the case of the nor'easter, this was disappointing as evidence for the existence of the Great Lakes storm was followed by the realization that it could not have produced the weather responsible for the tragic event.

Putting the Pieces Together

While the main goal of collecting weather information for October 31, 1780, was to determine the reason why the *Ontario* went down, there was another step to take before many of the questions could be answered. The newly uncovered information had to be plotted on a map. This would result in a crude, but fairly reliable weather map for the days leading up to, and including, the fateful day when the *Ontario* disappeared under the waves of Lake Ontario.

It can be stated with fairly high confidence that on October 31, one storm system was found in the vicinity of Lake Huron, while a second storm system was developing off the North Carolina coast. It is also evident that a strong area of high pressure was anchored over Quebec. During the course of the afternoon and evening, energy from the Great Lakes storm would move to the Mid Atlantic coast where it would greatly enhance the secondary storm that was also feeding upon the warm waters of the Gulf Stream. The intensifying coastal storm would generate strong winds and a wealth of precipitation, including accumulating snows found well inland from the coast.

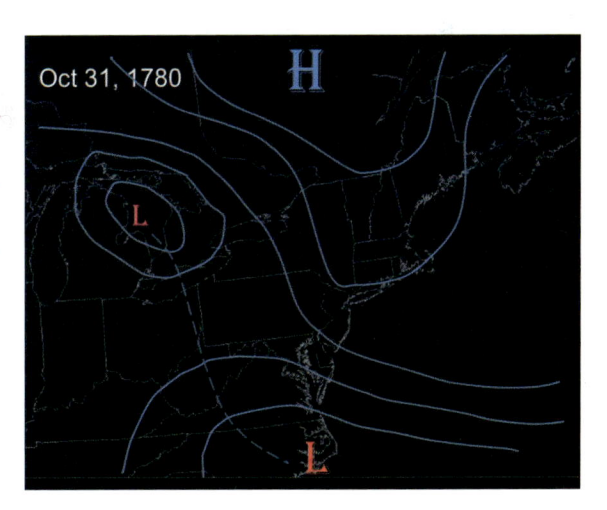

Image courtesy of Bob Hamilton

The information supplied by the British fleet on the north side of Long Island strongly suggests that the coastal storm would have then be held in place for two to three days by blocking high pressure to its north. This would keep relatively strong winds along the Mid Atlantic coast but would do little in generating significant weather over Lake Ontario. It would, however, support a southward push of cold air across the lake. This revelation spawned a new theory.

It is common during the late summer and fall to have chilly air create unstable conditions over the relatively warm waters of the Lower Great Lakes. In fact, this is one of the primary lifting mechanisms that contribute to lake-effect precipitation. If the environment over the lake is unstable enough within a favorable wind field, then the resulting thermals of rising air could encourage the development of waterspouts. A ship that would encounter such a waterspout at night would not have any warning and would almost certainly be capsized. The problem is that the synoptic conditions in this case would not have been favorable for waterspouts to develop. The thermal environment would have been similar to lake-effect snows that impact the Niagara Peninsula (southernmost Ontario), where warmer air aloft prevents the clouds from growing vertically. A relatively tall cloud is not only needed to generate significant lake-effect precipitation, but it is also necessary to support the development of a waterspout.

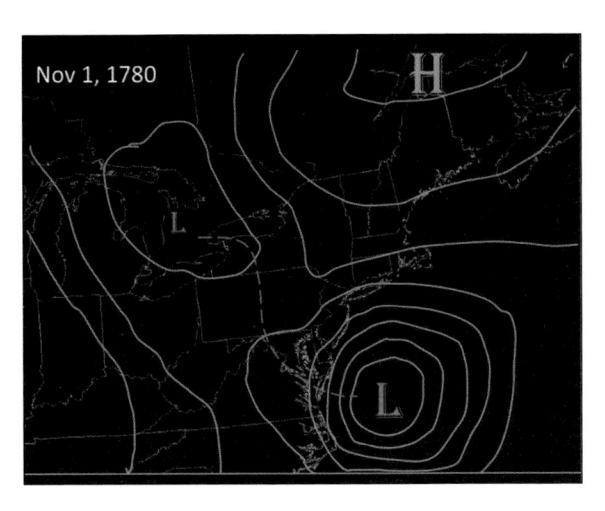

Image courtesy of Bob Hamilton

Image courtesy of Bob Hamilton

While the meteorological evidence is strong enough to rule out the Great Hurricane of 1780, a strong Great Lakes storm, and even a waterspout, there is just not enough information conclusively to explain the fate of the *Ontario*. Nearly all plausible weather-related possibilities have been disproven. At this point, a little speculation has to be introduced into the known meteorological facts.

One must go back to the letters to General Haldimand that spoke of a "sudden, violent storm from the Northeast." What could have possibly generated these surprise conditions? It would have taken a squall line of some kind, but one that would have come with little or no warning.

A northeast to southwest moving cold front, often referred to as a backdoor cold front, could have provided these conditions. Research has shown that the highest frequency for these types of fronts over the northeastern United States and Lower Great Lakes is during the early autumn months, with a peak in October. Temperatures can drop 25° F in just two hours with 30-to-40 knot winds not uncommon. The warmer waters of Lake Ontario at this time of year would enhance the instability of the air mass over the lake, and this would further enhance the significance of the frontal passage. Interestingly, backdoor cold fronts do not typically generate strong enough convection for thunderstorms to develop, so there would be no way for sailors at night to recognize the approaching hazard.

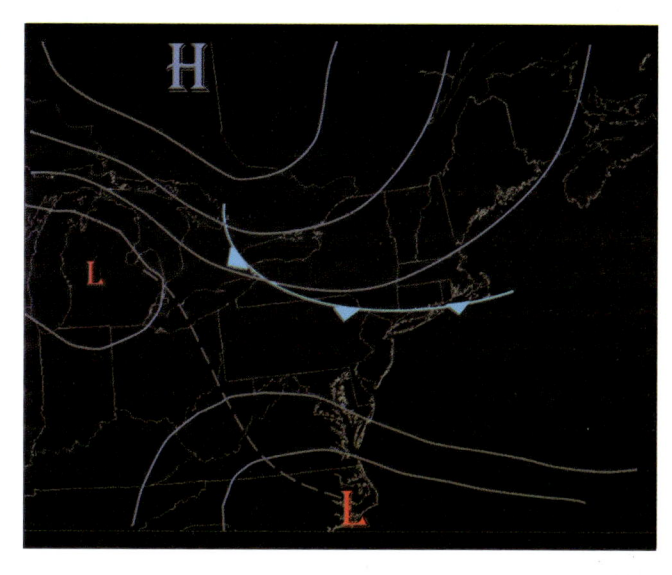

October 31, 1780 with showing front.
Image courtesy of Bob Hamilton

If winds would have shifted as much as 180 degrees with such a frontal passage while gusting to 30 to 40 knots, it is not hard to envision a skeleton crew panicking on deck. It would have been pitch black with no lightning or thunder to give any warning, and as the ship lurched, the startled crew could have overreacted — only exacerbating the dire situation. Recovery would then become impossible, as cannons would break loose and slam into the port side of the ship, sealing the fate of the ship.

Robert Hamilton is the Winter Weather Program Meteorologist at the National Weather Service in Buffalo, New York.

ONTARIO
A MODEL, BUILT AT 1:48 SCALE

By Ray Peacock

THE DRAFT

The Admiralty Collection of Ship Plans at the National Maritime Museum, Greenwich, London, holds the largest single collection of original ship plans in the world, with one million plans dating from the early 18th century to the present day.

The *Ontario* draft, or plan, shows three views of the vessel: the sheer plan with inboard detail (as seen from the side), the longitudinal half-breadth (as seen from above), and the body plan (seen from aft and fore,) with an ornate stern board outline.

Printed in Master Shipwright and Ship Builder John Coleman's writing is the title:

A Draught of the *"Ontario"* Launched at Carleton Island — the 10 May 1780 a statement which indicates the drawing was made after *Ontario* was built.

As is usual on drafts, Coleman also writes the designed dimensions as:

Length on lower deck — 80 feet
  Of the keel for tonnage — 64 feet 8 5/8"
Breadth extreme — 25 feet 4"
Draft in hold — 9 ft 0"
Burthen in tons — 226 55/94" (This is a volumetric measure of the cargo capacity of a ship)

A separate statement of the designed armament is added:
  Guns — 16...6 pounders, 6...4 Do.

The draught is drawn at a scale of 1:48, 1 inch: to 4 feet, the principal scale used for ships' drafts in the collection. (See *Ontario* admiralty drawing on page 58).

CONSTRUCTION FEATURES

As is usual, most elements that are common or defined by the various Admiralty "establishments" are omitted from drafts. Any subsequent changes to the original draft made by the designer were shown in color, either red or green. In the case of *Ontario*, the changes or additions, shown in red, include the location of the two decks, the upper extension of the rudder showing some detail of a rudder head, the inclusion of the companionway ladders fore and aft, the inclusion of two large breast hooks and the partitions in the hold, the position of the windlass and its supporting carrick bitts seated on a beam under the gun deck, and the belfry. No deck details are shown on the half-breadth plan, leaving the particulars to be fairly standardized. The shape of the hull at the deck, waterline and one other waterline, shows the vessel to be quite bluff at the bow, and full bodied towards the stern, consistent with its duties as a freight carrier more than a fast sailing ship. There is little dead-rise, indicating a designed ability to take groundings.

There remained a degree of speculation on several major points. The draft shows *Ontario* clearly to be a brig, a vessel with two masts, square rigged on the fore and mainmast, with a spanker or driver on the aft side of the mainmast. Anecdotally however, *Ontario* may have been a snow — a larger vessel than a brig, square rigged on the foremast and the main topmast, and with a large driver, the gaff jaws of which are mounted to a snow mast. A snow mast, or trysail mast, is a small mast located directly behind the mainmast, stepped on the deck and secured at its upper end near the fighting top. In view of such a major modification, why did Coleman omit this significant alteration to the drawing? Perhaps Captain Andrews made the modification later as a result of experiencing sail-handling on such a large vessel was facilitated by converting her to a snow.

The sheer plan shows the main gun deck ports — 8 per side — accounting for the "16 six-pounders" on the gun deck, although the forward-most port did not usually have a permanent gun because of the requirement for crew accommodation. The two "extra" six-pounders would be used as bow- or stern-chasers on the foc's'le or the quarter deck, and the six four pounders would be located four on the quarter deck and two on the forecastle.

The elm tree pumps, which remove water draining to the bilges, are prominent on the draft, while the companion-way ladders give access below from the forecastle and quarter decks. A handrail or covered housing is shown above the quarter deck companion.

Deck beams for both decks are clearly shown, and there is a longitudinal raised section on the upper deck, indicating a coaming, scaled to about 9" high, which is probably the length of the main hatchway. The width dimension of this main waist hatch, which would normally be delineated by gangways on either side, is not shown on the longitudinal half breadth plan.

The crew accommodation would be under the fo'c'sle on the gun deck, a space which would be very crowded. There is no indication of a galley, but one would have been located here. The sick berth would be positioned here, together possibly with a manger for live animals, with a couple of four-pounder guns stowed along the bulwarks.

Partitions on the gun deck, one forward of the mainmast, the other midway to the captain's cabin, delineate commissioned officers quarters. Two partitions fore and aft of the mainmast are shown in the hold, and a partition with a light deck below the captain's cabin, accessed by a grating-covered "booby hatch," allows access to the stern and rudder timbers.

Access in the hold to a partitioned space accommodating the magazine near the bow beneath the main gun deck is through a small hatch on the gun deck. Access to the main hold is by a grating-covered hatch located midway along the gun deck, immediately in front of the mast, and while a ladder is not shown, a movable one would have been required, probably the one visible in the jumble of timbers near the bow when found. Loading long cargo into the hold would be difficult at the midships position, and access ports would conventionally be cut into the lower counter for this.

A pair of fenders, which protect the sides of the ship when loading cargo, is shown. Entryway steps on the outside of the hull are not drawn, but their position is conventionally just forward of the mainmast.

Ships of this size, and even larger, would be maneuvered in port, and, in the absence of wind, in open waters, by oars or sweeps, manned by the crew. Although not shown on the draft I have added these, with their characteristic horizontal horseshoe-shaped hinges, along the sides of the hull.

Notable is the height of the bulwarks above the upper deck in the waist and forward to the bow — only about one foot — requiring considerable care when moving between the quarterdeck and fo'c'sle. Two posts are shown, one forward of the break of the quarter deck and the other at the forward companionway steps. A rope strung between these would be a safety feature, or they might be crutches for spare spars, which were often carried on naval vessels, and thus serving a dual purpose.

How was *Ontario* steered, by a tiller or by steering wheel? No indication is given on the draft, but while the ship's wheel initially came into use in about 1715, the projection of the rudder head above the quarterdeck suggests that a tiller was indeed fitted.

Many conventional design features were developed and built into the hull of the model (see image labeled "Hull before discovery of *Ontario*") before I had the privilege of seeing the 90-minute video taken from the

ROV when Jim Kennard and Dan Scoville found *Ontario*, "somewhere between Niagara and Rochester."

MODEL STYLE

I decided from the outset that the model should be as close to a definitive version as possible, consistent with the selected model style. There are several building styles which I might have chosen, such as solid, fully planked, plank on bulkhead, and half model on a decorative backboard. However, I have always admired the classical "Admiralty" models of the 17th and 18th Centuries, a stylized variation on the plank-on-frame model mandated by the Admiralty in 1716, to accompany shipbuilding proposals. This shows the form of the hull in the un-planked frames below the main wale, and planked above, often with decks partially planked to show the structure below decks, and usually without masts and spars. Despite warnings from friends about the complexity of building such a model, I decided to go ahead, at a scale of ¼ inch to 1 foot. Further, I wanted to use as little paint on the model as possible, using different woods to produce an attractive model.

LINES ACCURACY

Over time, paper undergoes dimensional changes, which in turn results in distortion of the lines. It was, therefore, first necessary to check that the lines on the draft were true in all dimensional views; otherwise considerable trimming and adjustment would be required as construction progressed. The length dimension on my copy of the draft was 0.275" shorter than the scaled length, equivalent to a little over 13" actual, and the beam was 0.11" narrower than the scaled dimension, about 5" actual. In addition, there is evidence from other drafts that the actual ship, as built, would differ from the original design, depending on the availability of materials to build her to those lines, and how the various tradesmen interpreted the drawing. Also individual captains would often modify these structures after experiencing the ship under sail.

DERIVATION OF FRAME SHAPES

To make an accurate model, I first made a half model, using the dimensions on the draft scaled accurately to 1:48, adjusting (reducing) the body plan width and sheer plan length proportionally, and fairing the model to

Half model on backboard

correct the lines plans. In today's world, fairing the lines from the draft can be done by the application of computer-assisted drawing software, but when I started to model *Ontario*, this software was very expensive and I could not justify its purchase, nor the time to learn to use it.

I first mounted the half model on a back-board, and then used an apparatus constructed from ¼" acrylic, which allows a pointer to travel in vertically and horizontally to follow the shape of the hull at specified intervals.

This pointer movement transfers to a pencil, which traces an exact copy of its path onto a sheet of card for each selected station. After the mechanism is moved to the next station location, the pointer traces the new shape onto another card. In this way, the faired shape of the hull at 5/16" intervals along its length is drawn on individual cards. These shapes are then used as patterns for the model frames. The distance between each frame on a full-size ship is only a few inches — and gives rise to the description of warships as having "wooden walls." But on Admiralty models, the distance between frames is widened so that the internal structures can be

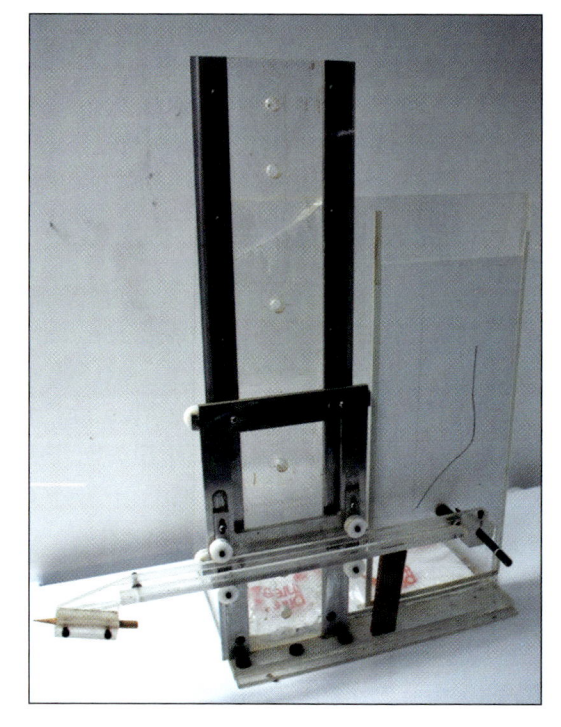

Frame-taking apparatus, pointer on left, pencil and card on right.

seen. This distance between one side of a frame and the corresponding next frame is called the "room and space." I selected a sistered frame thickness of 5/16" and a similar space of 5/16" to indicate the stoutness of *Ontario*'s construction required to endure the weight-carrying requirements of a freighter, the ability to withstand the crush of ice in winter, and to resist the strain of accidental grounding in the shallow reaches of the Upper St. Lawrence.

MODEL BUILDING MATERIALS AND METHODS

The classic model building wood is European boxwood, which is bright yellow and slowly matures to a rich golden color. However, I had a source of a similar wood called degamè, also known as lemonwood and lancewood, which is slightly darker in color but has all the same properties of hardness with a very close, almost invisible, grain. This was the principal wood used, with rails and trim in Swiss pear and boxwood, and holly for the deck. The main wale is ebony. All joints are reinforced with trunnels made from bamboo at 0.022" diameter (equivalent to 1" at scale). After sizing the wood to exact dimensions, it was finished with grain filler and sanded smooth to a semi-matt finish. The use of different varieties of wood allowed me to "paint with wood;" the only actual paint used is red acrylic paint on the inside of the bulwarks and the gun ports.

Metal parts such as the chains, pintles and gudgeons on the rudder, hinges for the gun-port covers, eyebolts in the deck and other places, and the anchors, are made from brass. I turned the guns individually from brass on my miniature lathe, fitting each one to its wheeled carriage and rigged with controlling ropes as on the full-size gun. All brass parts are chemically blackened. There are about eight diameters of rope used on *Ontario*, all of which are made on my miniature rope walk. Blocks used for these lines are made from boxwood. The ends of the catheads are fitted with rotating sheaves for raising and lowering the anchors.

I constructed the model by the "upside down" method pioneered by Harold Hahn. This essentially erects frames upside down in a building jig, which acts as a solid base and a reference point from which to take measurements, while keeping the frames square, rigid, and in place. Frames, or "ribs," are made from a group of futtocks which, when assembled, form the rounded shape of the hull. The framing wood is first dimensioned to the width and thickness of a half frame, and individual pieces which make up each frame (which will eventually become the futtocks) are cut and assembled to make half-frame blanks.

Each half of the frame blank, the futtock pieces of which overlap the joints in its twin half, is then glued and "trunnelled" (pinned) to its twin to make a strong double "sistered" frame. After marking the locations of the wales, the gun ports and other hull features determined from the draft, each sistered frame was cut to the pattern corresponding to its position in the body plan. The sistered frames are erected sequentially in the jig, and the keel, stem and stern pieces are added to make a hull structure which is rigid and remarkably strong.

The shelf, beams, planking of the gun deck, hatches, and other internal details, are fitted while the hull remains in the jig. The hull is then cut from the jig and mounted on a baseboard right-side up, and can be worked on for the rest of the construction.

THE DISCOVERY AND "AS BUILT" CHANGES

The hull was almost complete.
Then came the news that *Ontario* had been found!
I immediately contacted Jim Kennard who graciously invited me to view the video of the discovered ship that he and Dan Scoville had made. My notes when I saw the video indicated areas where the "as built" ship differed from the model.

The ship is colonized by zebra and quagga mussels which conceal much of the detail. The billet head carved in the shape of a fiddle head, shown on

Hull before discovery of *Ontario*.

the draft, was an immediate, but not unique, identifier of *Ontario*. All rope fibers have completely perished, and spars which were supported by them, have fallen and are scattered around the hull. A 21-foot longboat, which was the first target seen on the ROV some distance away, is in remarkably good condition, having only a relatively small amount of damage to the starboard bow planking. A smaller 16'6" cutter is lying alongside the port quarter, wrecked and crushed by the inclined hull.

The fore and mainmasts are standing vertical, and the upper masts are still in position. A snow mast stands behind the mainmast but further aft than would be expected. A swan-necked tiller is in place, jammed hard over to the port side by an upset gun. Other guns are present, appearing to be smaller than a typical six-pounder of the period — probably four-pounders. It was not unusual for such fittings as guns to be salvaged from other vessels or locations, and the ship designer's gun sizes may not therefore be fully accommodated

A two-decker the size of *Ontario* would generally have narrow gangways, two to three feet wide, on either side of the ship connecting the quarterdeck with the forecastle. This would set the pattern of the butt joints on the rest of the deck planking, and the resulting trunnel pattern. For strength reasons, the butts in planking were required to be three or four plank widths apart when they land on the same beam. I framed and planked the upper deck with this feature and these dimensions, resulting in an open waist area in the upper deck about 16 feet wide (4" at scale), and 24 feet long (6" at scale). This would allow rapid clearing of smoke from guns on the deck below.

However, most prominently, the waist opening on the upper deck of the ship is considerably narrower but longer than would conventionally be constructed, a major difference seen when comparing my original upper deck and the final construction. The result is a full upper deck with a long cargo hatch, rather than separate fo'c'sle and quarterdecks connected by gangways. The hatch in the waist on the actual ship is considerably narrower and shorter than my initial conventional design, and estimated to be 6 feet by 21 feet (1½" by 5¼" at scale). In addition, the Haldimand Papers, written at the time of the loss of the ship, describe the finding of gratings on shore. A wide open waist would not have been covered with gratings, but gratings would have been used to cover a narrow-hatch waist, therefore affording a full deck while allowing some, but not as much, ventilation of the deck below.

The time came, therefore, to take the proverbial chainsaw to the model, to make major changes to ensure accuracy of the model. The actual open section is narrower (approx. 1½" not 4"), and shorter (approx. 5¼" not 7¼") than the original construction. (These differences can be compared in the prior image, "Hull before discovery of *Ontario*" and the last image in the chapter "*Ontario*, hull complete, as found, deck planking adjusted".) This change required not merely making a smaller aperture, framed with coamings, but a complete replacement of the mid-ships deck planking — because of the changed plank butt pattern and the location of trunnels. (I did ask Jim to find his next shipwreck <u>before</u> I started to make a model of it). I also constructed gratings to fit over this opening, omitting a section at the aft end for visual access below. (I also left some planking off amidships and on the quarterdeck for the same reason.)

The decorative transom board is shown in some detail on the draft and is clearly visible on the ship. This, combined with the billet head, confirms the identity of *Ontario*. All the window frames in my original construction of the stern galleries were glazed, using microscope cover slides, with strips of holly for the mullions. On the video it is clear that the outermost starboard window on the stern gallery is solid, not glass. This would be consistent with affording privacy to the captain's heads, which would be located here.

Bow, showing billboard at chains, cathead end plate.

Protection of the side planking at the bow from damage caused by catting and fishing the anchor is a little unusual. Instead of sacrificial anchor lining planking lying immediately against the side planking and forward of the foremost shroud, a billboard is mounted at an angle proud of the side planking, from the top of the wale to the outer edge of the forward channel. (This also gives an indication of the length of the shank of the anchors.)

The vulnerable end-grain of the cathead timber was typically protected by a wooden block, the face of which is carved in the shape of a decorative cat's head, hence the name. In the case of *Ontario* however, the pattern of the carving is several concentric rings. Noticeably it has no zebra mussel growth on it, and given the pesticide properties of copper-containing compounds, it is likely that this plate is made from a copper-containing alloy such as brass or bronze.

Similarly a cleat on the mainmast is mussel-free and likely made from bronze. Might other cleats be of a similar material?

The aft companionway is protected by a handrail on three sides, not by a covered construction. This would have been enclosed, when required, by a temporary canvas cover as shelter for the stairs from the elements. I originally built the small deckhouse (visible in figure labeled "Hull before discovery of *Ontario*"), but this has now been consigned to the "next model" box.

I installed a binnacle box in front of the tiller, containing a compass and two illuminating lamps. The glazed skylight unit to give light to the cabins under the quarterdeck has also now been consigned to the "next model" box.

I researched such details as cabin locations on the gun deck before adding the upper deck, and determined the location of partitions for officers' cabin locations on the gun deck. I placed only wood strips on the deck here so that they would not obscure the gun locations. I also made a stove and mounted it on a fire-brick base in the already crowded crew quarters under the fo'c'sle on the gun deck. I located a plate on the upper deck where a removable flue would have been positioned above it. I constructed two ship's boats that appear in the video, although a third is reported to have washed ashore the morning after the disaster.

The longboat represents the first ROV "target" and is 21 feet long, (5¼" at scale). The second is the cutter or jolly boat, 16 feet long, (4 1/8" at scale), being crushed on the starboard quarter.

Both boats are clinker built i.e. with overlapping planks, using principally holly, with Swiss pear trim, sole gratings, and blackened brass "iron"-work. They would have been fitted with masts, oars and sails when in use, and would probably have been towed when *Ontario* was under sail in order to reduce congestion on the deck.

21-foot longboat.

16-foot cutter.

Ontario: A Model, Built at 1:48 Scale

Ontario, as found.

Ontario, hull complete, as found, deck planking adjusted.

83

The image "*Ontario*, as found" shows the model of *Ontario* as she was discovered, with masts standing but unsupported by rigging. Fallen spars will not be added to the final display because the model will be presented fully rigged with the two small boats alongside.

Ontario is an attractive vessel. Researching and building this definitive model of such an historic ship, knowledge about which is so sparse, has given me much pleasure.

SOURCES:

Britton Smith, Arthur. *Legend of the Lake: The 22-Gun Brig Sloop* Ontario *1780*. New Discovery Edition. Kingston: Quarry Press, 1997, 2009.

Coleman, Jonathan. *Ontario (1780) Draft*. National Maritime Museum, Greenwich, London. http://collections.rmg.co.uk/collections/objects/84516.html#S1mXjpUTv5UhY1QJ.99

Goodwin, Peter. *The Construction and Fitting o the English Man of War, 1650–1850*. London: Conway Maritime Press, 1987.

Hahn, Harold M. *Ships of the American Revolution and Their Models*. London: Conway Maritime Press, 1988.

Lavery, Brian. *The Arming and Fitting of Ships of War, 1600–1815*. London: Conway Maritime Press, 1987.

May, W.E. *The Boats of Men of War*. Greenwich, London: National Maritime Museum, 1974. London: Chatham Publishing, 1999.

All photos by the author.

Ray Peacock was born and brought up in England near the River Mersey and the Manchester Ship Canal, where he developed an interest in the maritime world. Books from the local library were a source of his interest in the beauty of ships, although his adult career was principally in the food industry, where he became Vice President of an international food company. After arriving in Canada with his wife and three children in 1971 he bought a sailboat and gained experience in the art of sailing and the practicalities of ship design in his spare time. Before and since retiring from the corporate world Ray builds models from original plans, and has restored many models for clubs and private individuals. His research into the history of the period of the subject models, and the reproduction of their design and building methods, using appropriate tools and techniques, advances his knowledge of the miniature ship-building world in the quest to produce the definitive model.

The Later Years
2008–2018

Unexpected Rare Shipwreck Discovery: A Daggerboard Schooner

After our discovery of the *Ontario*, Dan and I set our sights on locating the largest ship to have foundered in Lake Ontario, the 253-foot steel steamship, *Nisbet Grammer*. It was late in the fall of the 2008 season and we figured that this would be the last trip out for the year. It was a rough day on the lake as waves increased in height as the hours passed. We were making long survey runs in water depths between 400 and 500 feet towing a side-scan sonar towfish connected to nearly 2,000 feet of cable. When towing this much cable, you have to make the runs long with as few turns as possible as it may take over a mile to make each turn. All the time, we are watching the sonar monitor very carefully to make sure that the towfish does not hit the bottom. As the waves increased to three and four feet and the boat drove into them, the cable jerked with each crashing wave. Suddenly, a target appeared on the sonar screen that was almost immediately followed by a gap in the recording process. Then the signal returned, followed by another gap in the recording. We assumed there was an intermittent problem with the cable. The jerking of the cable was causing a loss of the sonar return signal due to a failing electrical connection. We couldn't continue in the same direction any longer but we thought that if we turned around and powered through the lake with the waves at our stern that, just maybe, going back with the waves to the target location, the cable would not be as stressed and would not lose the signal as often. We turned the boat around and headed back along a similar course line. The sonar signal was occasionally compromised but held up until just past the target that we had previously seen. With two track lines recorded in opposing directions, I could determine a fairly good position of the target that we had just observed. Even though it was late in the season, two weeks later the lake was calm with light winds, so we returned and deployed Dan's ROV to explore the shipwreck.

The shipwreck is upright and in remarkable condition considering it plunged over 500 feet to its final resting place on the bottom. The ROV landed on the ship in the area where the cabin would have been. Only a few posts that held up the cabin structure remain. This area is void of any items such as a stove, furniture, or other materials. A rail wraps around the starboard and port side at the level of cabin roof, which also served as an upper deck. At the stern are the remains of the rudder trunk between two small

Unexpected Rare Shipwreck Discovery: A Daggerboard Schooner

Unknown daggerboard schooner. Watercolor by Roland E. Stevens III

windows about 20 inches square. The stern rail has an artistically pleasing scrollwork feature. Moving forward, the ship's pump sits on the port side of the deck just forward of the area where the cabin would have been located. A few feet in front of the former entrance to the cabin, the stub of the mainmast can be seen protruding above the deck. Just forward of this mast stub is the opening for one of the two ship's holds, measuring approximately five feet in length by three-and-one-half feet wide. Between this hold and the forward hold appear to be two partitions that are in line with each other. Each partition was one-to-two inches thick by about four-and-one-half feet in length, and rises up from the deck three-and-one-half feet. Not until we researched further did we come to understand that we were looking at daggerboards that had been forced up into that position by the ship resting on the bottom of the lake. Next to and on the starboard side of the daggerboards and a few inches away is a long round pole covered with quagga mussels that stretches just beyond the length of the two daggerboards. We initially believed that this was part of the mechanical assembly that assisted in raising and lowering both daggerboards. Further viewing of the underwater video showed a rounded notch in the lip of both holds nearest to each daggerboard. We hypothesize that this pole-like object may have been placed over the top of the daggerboards and secured within the notches of each hold to prevent them from riding up above the deck when in use in open water.

Just beyond the forward hold is the stub of the foremast. Both the stubs of the main and foremast look as if they had been cut off approximately one foot above the deck. The bowsprit can be seen beginning only a few feet from the foremast and extends for 12 feet past the tip of the bow. Next to the port side of the shipwreck and adjacent to the forward hold there appears to be a cover-like object about the same length as the hold. It has not yet been clearly determined if this is a cover for a hold or something else. There were no anchors, winch, block and tackles, or deadeyes found on the shipwreck. The schooner was built without side rails or enclosures (bulwarks) on either side of the main deck, a characteristic of vessels built during the very early 1800s. The length of the schooner measures 55 feet long and 15 feet wide.

We have never been able to identify the schooner, as we could not find a documented account of a vessel of this type sinking in Lake Ontario. It appears from the video survey of the shipwreck that the schooner had been stripped of all useable items such as anchors, iron fittings, cabin with contents, and tiller. It is highly unlikely that this ship would have been transported many miles out into the middle of the lake to be scuttled. Another, more likely scenario may be that this schooner was in the process of being converted to a barge or other sailing craft by its owners. Perhaps it broke free from its moorings in the ice or during a violent storm and was carried far out into the lake where it eventually sank. Considering the ship's location and the typical prevailing northwest winds on Lake Ontario, it is possible that this ship came from the York (Toronto) area in the early 1800s. The other possibility is that it was being towed to another location when it foundered. The ship eventually sank probably due to a weak section below the starboard stern window, which is missing.

Through research and discussion with some of our shipwreck peers, we determined that this schooner is called a *daggerboard* schooner. Sailing vessels of this type were in use on the Lakes for only a short period of time beginning in the very early 1800s. When discovered, this ship was the only daggerboard schooner known to have been found in the Great Lakes. The daggerboard schooner was typically a small, shallow draft ship having one or more wood panels that could be extended through the keel to increase its effectiveness while underway in the open water. The purpose of daggerboards was to prevent the schooner from being pushed sideways when sailing windward or with the wind coming from one side (abeam) of the vessel. A single daggerboard was a panel of wood perhaps one to two inches thick and four to five feet long, surrounded by a narrow watertight enclosure. The daggerboard would be pushed squarely down though the bottom of the vessel to increase her draught while sailing and hauled up by tackles at either end. The ability to raise the daggerboards when entering a shallow harbor was a great advantage. The boat could load and unload personnel and cargo in all sorts of locations that would not otherwise be accessible with a larger sailing craft. The term "daggerboard" was also referred to as drop-keel, slip-keel, sliding-keel, barn-door, or center-plate.

The invention of the daggerboard or drop-keel is generally credited to British Captain John Schank in 1774; however, the early use of the daggerboard in sailing craft prior to the 1800s can actually be traced back to China and possibly South America. Captain Schank proposed and then adapted the daggerboard concept for use in the cutter *Trial*, built in Portsmouth, England, for the British Admiralty in 1790. This ship turned out to be a great success, as the *Trial* was able to out-sail most of the smaller cutters. In the next few years, the British followed up by building a ship-sloop, two classes of gun-brigs, and 16 brigs utilizing the daggerboard concept. Depending on the ship design, multiple daggerboards were utilized to compensate for the shifting of the vessel's center of gravity as the sails moved fore-and-aft. Ten years after the British Admiralty built the *Trial*, further interest in ships with daggerboards was put on hold due to the problem of making the enclosure for the daggerboards watertight.

As recounted by Captain James Van Cleve in his memoirs, the first vessel on the Great Lakes to utilize daggerboards was a skiff brought to Oswego from Niagara around 1806. In September 1813, Major-General James Wilkinson wrote in a letter to the US Secretary of War "... Before I left Sackets Harbor, I ordered a dozen slip-keeled boats to carry 50 men and row 30 oars to be armed with a light cannon in their bow." References can also be found in the 1813 transport dispatches of Buffalo army officers of the use of slip-keel (daggerboard) sailing vessels. From 1817 to 1820, sailing vessels on Lake Erie greatly increased in numbers, though not in size. These ships varied from 18 to 65 tons burden, and most of them utilized daggerboards. It is thought that by 1819, one or more ship builders in York (Toronto) were producing ships that utilized daggerboards. The pivoted centerboard was patented in 1811, and during the next several years, larger ships would employ this method of extending the functionality of the keel. By 1820, the daggerboard design gave way to that of the pivoted centerboard. It is reasonable to assume that many of the early daggerboard schooners, initially military vessels, were later used for the commercial transport of people and goods on both Lake Ontario and Lake Erie.

Although we were not successful that season in finding the *Nisbet Grammer*, we were extremely pleased to have made the discovery of a very rare Great Lakes vessel, a daggerboard schooner.

SOURCES:

Chapelle, Howard. *American Small Sailing Craft: their design, development and Construction.* New York: W.W. Norton & Co., 1951.

Chapelle, Howard. *The History of the American Sailing Navy.* New York: Bonanza Books, 1949.

Van Cleve, James. "Reminiscences of Early Steamboats, Propellers and Sailing Vessels on Lake Ontario and River St. Lawrence." Unpublished manuscript, 1877.

A Lucky Wind Makes for Discovery of the Schooner *C. Reeve*

The shipwreck search season on Lake Ontario typically starts in early May and lasts until the middle of October. Many long days are spent on the lake searching; in the off season, we spend countless hours building search equipment, maintaining the boat and trailer, and researching in the archives of various libraries. Our goal has always been to find at least one shipwreck per season, otherwise the search becomes too discouraging.

In 2005, when Dan and I began searching for shipwrecks in the western portion of Lake Ontario, many assumed that our first target would be the *Ontario*. It wasn't. Based on the research I had done, I estimated that the search area could be up to 600 square miles. Dan and I could never have covered that area in a six-month season, especially while we were still both working full time at Eastman Kodak Company. We chose instead a ship whose sinking had been covered by several newspapers in 1862, the schooner *C. Reeve*.[1] The search for this ship turned out to be much more difficult than we anticipated. From 2005 to 2009, we covered well over 200 square miles of western Lake Ontario looking for this ship. In the process, we found several other shipwrecks, including the salt ship *Milan* and the *Ontario*, both discussed in earlier chapters. So much for the "best-laid plans of mice and men."

Our initial discovery of the target was not made by the conventional search methods used previously. In early summer of 2009, while searching for the *C. Reeve*, we noticed a boat following us while we conducted our search grid. We had heard from some of our peers on the Upper Lakes that people will occasionally follow research teams like our own in an effort to learn the coordinates of a shipwreck. These "claim jumpers" apparently use the coordinates to announce "their" discovery without putting in the hard work and investment. That day, we pulled in our sonar equipment, headed further out into the lake, took a break for lunch and dared the spies to sit it out or go away. They went away and we continued our search. As evening approached, we decided to pack things up and head back to port. Meanwhile our boat had drifted, propelled by a light breeze. As luck would have

---

[1] Various research websites and publications list two versions of the name: *C. Reeve* or *C. Reeves*. This is a typical problem in 19th Century documentation of ship's names.

it, Dan glanced over at the depth recorder just as the wind was taking the boat for a ride right over the top of a shipwreck. The position was quickly noted for a return trip. In August, we revisited the site and deployed Dan's ROV to complete an underwater survey with hopes of confirming the identity of the shipwreck we had discovered by simple chance.

The depth where this shipwreck lies has no natural light. We relied on Dan's ROV with cameras and high-intensity lighting to bring back images of the sunken vessel. The shipwreck is sitting upright on the bottom and entirely encrusted with quagga mussels. The mainmast still stands but the foremast, snapped at its base, lies off to the port side with only a few feet resting on the port railing. The ROV video revealed significant damage to the starboard side of the hull approximately 35 feet from the bow and near where the foremast would have stood. There are many spars lying at various angles across the deck, as well as numerous deadeyes and block and tackles. There are many large pieces of what appear to be thick rope lying about the deck. Both of the anchors lie half buried in the soft bottom off the bow. The hatches of the cargo holds are still tightly closed. The cabin is fairly large and stretches completely across the deck, from one side of the ship rail to the other. The mainmast boom is lying right across the cabin entrance and on top of the cabin roof. At the stern of the schooner there is

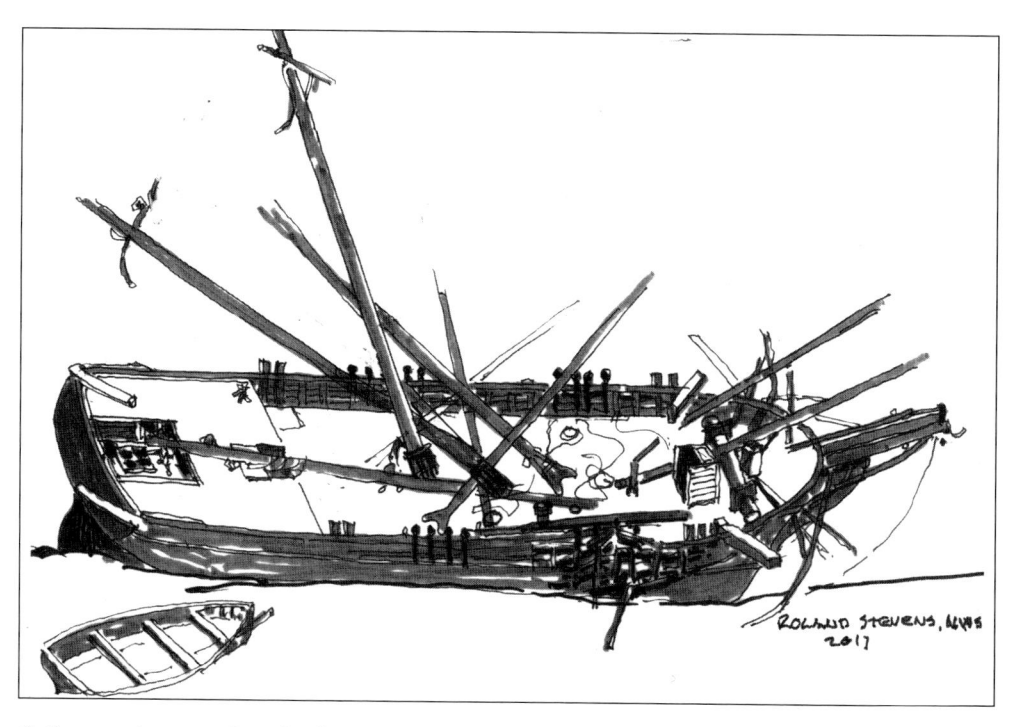

C. Reeve underwater. Drawing by Roland E. Stevens III

an open area cut out of the cabin where the ship's wheel and steering mechanism are located. The steering arrangement appears quite different from schooners we have observed before. In this area, a door to the main cabin, partially opened, is half buried in decades of deposited silt. On the port side, off the stern, a long boat is seen resting on the lake bottom.

The schooner that Dan and I found did not have an observable name painted on the stern of the ship, but other clues were available to identify the vessel. This shipwreck had two masts and the starboard side of the hull was extensively damaged suggesting some type of collision. The general location of this shipwreck was consistent with the accident report of a collision between two vessels off Oak Orchard in 1862. Measurements made by a sector-scanning sonar mounted on the underwater ROV showed a length of 119 feet and a beam of 26 feet. Only one possible candidate matched each piece of evidence our survey had produced, the schooner *C. Reeve*.

The *C. Reeve* was a two-masted gaff rigged schooner built in 1853 by the firm of B.B. & N. Jones in Buffalo for Nathan Reeve and his new business, the Detroit and Newburgh Line, to haul lumber. During the nine years that the schooner was operating on the Great Lakes, she sustained a few minor collisions, lost her masts once in her first season, and was driven ashore in a storm at Mackinac, Michigan. In July 1858, the *Reeve* made a trans-Atlantic crossing when she sailed from Detroit, Michigan, to Liverpool, England, with a cargo of black walnut lumber. In October of that same year, the *Reeve* returned with a full load of crockery.

The *C. Reeve* departed Chicago with a cargo of 13,500 bushels of corn destined for Oswego, New York, in the second half of November 1862. On the fateful night of Saturday, November 22, the *Reeve* had made it to Lake Ontario and was continuing to sail east toward her final port. The schooner *Exchange* was headed west on the lake for the Welland Canal. The *Exchange* had cleared the port of Oswego the previous day with a load of 2,000 barrels of Onondaga salt bound for ports on Lake Erie. In the early evening hours, a blinding snowstorm set in over Lake Ontario with a strong wind coming out of the north. Visibility was almost nonexistent and neither crew from the *C. Reeve* or the *Exchange* could see ahead. In a short time, the *Exchange* collided with the *Reeve* on her starboard side, just aft of the foremast. The accident occurred off the port of Oak Orchard, New York.

The *Exchange* plowed right into the rigging that secured the *Reeve*'s foremast to the starboard side of the ship. This caused the foremast to lose all support and it immediately toppled over. The collision also created a large gap in the side of the *Reeve*'s hull, allowing water to pour into the schooner. Within a few minutes, the *Reeve* sank out of sight into the depths of Lake Ontario. The *Exchange* was not without significant damage; she lost her bowsprit, which became tangled in the *Reeve*'s foremast rigging. She also sustained severe damage to her cutwater, the forward portion of the stem which cuts through the water. Leaking but still afloat, the *Exchange* took onboard the crew of the *C. Reeve*, then turned about and headed for the port of Rochester. The crew of the *Reeve* only had enough time to save themselves and consequently lost all their personal effects. *The Rochester Union and Advertiser* described the condition of the *Exchange* after returning to port reporting, "She bears the marks of a collision and reminds one of a bully with his nose badly broken."

Shipwrecks are fascinating for any number of reasons. The number of Great Lakes vessels that have made a trans-Atlantic crossing prior to the opening of the Seaway in 1959, is fractional. To have discovered one that sank in Lake Ontario after that famous crossing is especially rewarding.

SOURCES:

Rochester Union and Advertiser, November 24, 1862.
_____, November 25, 1862.
_____, November 26, 1862.

Queen of the Lakes

Queen of the Lakes.   Watercolor by Roland E. Stevens III

In August 2009, our shipwreck search team consisting of Dan, Roland, and myself began searching for shipwrecks off Sodus Point, New York, when the stunning image of a three-masted schooner appeared on the screen of the DeepVision side-scan sonar system. That season we began using this new sonar system which projected the side-scan image onto a computer screen instead of printing it out on paper. Like so many of the wrecks our team has discovered over the past few years, this target was well beyond the depth limits of recreational diving. When we discover a target like this, we want to get the ROV down to the wreck site as quickly as possible because there is no better feeling than seeing clear, distinct images of a virgin shipwreck transmitted to the top-side monitor. Unfortunately, Dan's ROV was in Houston as Dan had relocated there after accepting a position with Oceaneering International. We were hopeful that Dan would return during the 2010 season with the ROV to obtain video of the shipwreck but national events would dictate otherwise. In 2010, the Deepwater Horizon oil disaster forced Dan to change his shipwreck search plans. As one of the lead project engineers on the repair team, Dan worked over 80 hours a week for four months to build the tools BP needed to fix the oil leak in the Gulf of Mexico. Our search team would have to wait another year and we could only imagine what this schooner would look like through the lens of the ROV video camera.

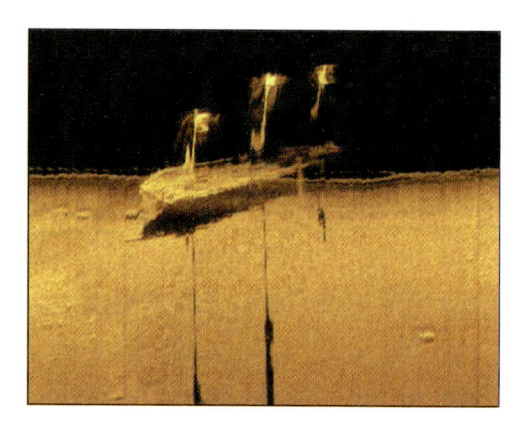

Side-scan sonar image of *Queen of the Lakes*.
Image courtesy of Jim Kennard

At long last Dan returned in 2011 with his underwater ROV and we deployed it over our new find during a calm day the first week in July. The initial images of the ship revealed the stern and a large rudder. On either side of the stern, the davits that had once held the yawl extend out and away from the ship. Moving upward and onto the deck, the ship's wheel is present. Behind the wheel are the remains of the ship's cabin; the roof has fallen into the area where the cabin once stood

Queen of the Lakes rudder.
Image courtesy of Jill Heinerth

making it difficult to see the contents. A round cylindrical-shaped object covered with quagga mussels, possibly a toilet, crock, or stove, protrudes from the roof debris. The water clarity permitted about 75 feet of visibility, which was enough

Queen of the Lakes wheel.
Image courtesy of Jill Heinerth

to view two of the standing masts with just barely a glimpse of the third (forward) mast from the vantage point of the stern cabin. On the deck are bundles of rope, or more likely cables, that were attached to the masts as standing rigging when she sank. Cables began replacing ropes for this purpose in the late 1800s. There are several holds along the deck where cargo would have been stored. All that is visible now is the silt that has filled each of the holds up to the deck.

Queen of the Lakes mast.
Image courtesy of Jill Heinerth

Queen of the Lakes anchor.
Image courtesy of Jill Heinerth

Approaching the bow, a donkey boiler sits on the forward deck. Up at the bow, the anchors of the schooner are still firmly secured in place. Using our tried and true method of identifying shipwrecks through survey data matched against historical records, we concluded this wreck is the *Queen of the Lakes*. During her career of 50 plus years, the *Queen of the Lakes* was one of the largest schooners operating on Lake Ontario.

The *Queen of the Lakes*, originally named the *Robert Taylor*, was built in the Portsmouth, Ontario shipyard in 1853. The ship registration records show that sometime prior to 1864, the ship was given her new name. Initially, the *Queen of the Lakes* was a two-masted schooner with a length of nearly 129 feet and a beam of 23 feet. In 1884, she came ashore and was damaged near Avon Point in Lake Erie. Two years later, she incurred major damage after being

Queen of the Lakes.   Image courtesy of the Historical Collection of the
Great Lakes at Bowling Green State University

wrecked near Brighton, Ontario. In 1887, Richardson & Sons of Kingston rebuilt her and added the third mast.[1]

In late November 1906, the *Queen of the Lakes* brought a load of feldspar (mineral-rock) from Kingston, Ontario, to the port of Charlotte (Rochester, New York). For the return trip, the schooner picked up a load of

---

[1] Registration records of Great Lakes vessels have been digitized into searchable websites. Sometimes the data is entered into these databases inaccurately resulting in conflicts on dates and dimensions. There are some inconsistencies with respect to the *Queen of the Lakes* between these different databases.

480 tons of coal and departed Charlotte for Kingston in the early evening of November 28 with a crew of six men. This was the last scheduled trip of the season. It was a cold November day with a strong wind blowing from the northwest. Within a few hours the winds shifted north and then northeast becoming gale force. The vessel began to leak badly. By midnight the *Queen of the Lakes* could not proceed on course to Kingston any longer. Three different times the water put out the fire in the boiler that worked the pumps. Water rushed in faster than the compromised pumps could hope to expel. Captain Chauncey Daryaw turned the *Queen of the Lakes* about and headed for Sodus Point, the nearest port, in order to save the ship and its crew. But it was not to be. The captain ordered the yawl to be made ready and the crew to abandon the ship. One member of the crew, however, failed to hear the orders. The old cook had fallen asleep and was still in his bunk. Captain Daryaw raced back to the cabin and woke the cook who, thinking that they had arrived back in Kingston, told the Captain to, "Wait till I put on my collar and tie" before leaving the boat. In his haste to get everyone off the ship, Captain Daryaw failed to retrieve his Masonic ring and his prized violin. When the crew in the yawl were less than 50 feet away from the schooner, the *Queen of the Lakes* disappeared into the depths of Lake Ontario.

The six-man crew had abandoned the sinking ship after midnight. The lake was tumultuous that night and the men struggled to keep the yawl from overturning. The captain had retrieved a cooking dish which was used to bail water from the yawl. The cold winds were very strong and the temperature continued to drop at a rapid rate. The crew battled the seas and the late November gale for a couple of hours. After rowing nearly 15 miles, they landed in the area of Chimney Bluffs. At 2:30 a.m. they found refuge at the home of Dana Waldron, a North Huron farmer, who took the shipwrecked sailors in, providing them with dry clothes and a warm meal. In the morning, they were transported to Lake Bluff and then on to Sodus Point. Unfortunately, the ship's owners, Richardson & Sons, had not insured the vessel or the cargo resulting in a total loss of $6,700. Captain Daryaw continued sailing on the Lakes for many more years until he passed away in 1922.

Discovering a shipwreck inevitably leads to the public getting a better understanding of the dangers of commercial maritime transportation. The story of the loss of the *Queen of the Lakes* — and that of the almost comical old cook, oblivious to the perilous situation — is a reminder to us all that foolishness maybe an acceptable excuse, but only when someone saves you so that you can offer that excuse.

Sources:

Cato Citizen, December 8, 1906.
Lake Shore News [Wolcott, New York], December 6, 1906.
Oswego Daily Times, November 30, 1906.
Palmer, Richard. "On the Waterfront: Maritime Life in Oswego and Lake Ontario," Regular column. *Palladium Times*, 2012.
Sodus Record, November 30, 1905.

In September 2018 professional underwater photographer Jill Heinerth along with Teddy Garlock made technical dives on the *Queen of the Lakes* to capture the most recent imagery of these shipwrecks.

TRAGEDY IN A NOVEMBER GALE

As the reader works through this book, it is clear that the clues necessary for finding a shipwreck can come from many different sources. Primary source documents, secondary published sources, personal memory, and even the work of other shipwreck hunters can be the difference between a season of fruitless searching or a season of success. The discovery and identification of the wreck described in this chapter owes its source to the unintentional work of the Canadian government.

In the mid-1990s, a Canadian geological survey team was on an expedition to locate underwater fissures in Lake Ontario. While searching one of the deepest depths of the lake off Sodus Point, the shape of a shipwreck appeared on their sonar screen. In the early summer 1997, the team returned on the HCMS *Cormorant*, a diving support vessel of the Royal Canadian Navy, to survey the shipwreck they discovered. The *Cormorant* was equipped with an SDL-1 submersible, a two-man submarine capable of reaching depths to 2,000 feet. The survey team knew this was a shipwreck but its type was still a mystery when they launched the SDL-1 into action.

When the submersible was near the lake bottom, the shape of a ship appeared on the sector-scanning

HMCS *Cormorant* deploying the SDL-1.
Image courtesy of Canadian Forces

sonar screen. (This display is very similar to that of a radar screen.) With the image of the ship centered in the middle of the screen, the displayed range rings gave an approximate indication that the shipwreck was nearly 140 feet in length. In the mid-90s, the visibility in Lake Ontario was not as good as it is today, so the range for seeing an object clearly was often limited to less than 10 feet. The submersible had to move in very close to identify what type of ship they had found. They initially approached the shipwreck from about mid ship on the port side and when it was in view, they reported their findings to the SDL command ship. "We have found the wreck, depth six eight one, and it is an old sailboat, wooden hull — now proceeding along the side." The reply from the topside crew was, "You

Isaac G. Jenkins underwater. Underwater images (L-R): Wheel, anchor on starboard bow, and cabin window.
Watercolor by Roland E. Stevens III
Images courtesy of Geological Survey of Canada, Natural Resources Canada

found the wrong wreck." Prior to the deployment of the manned submersible, some of the researchers thought their target might be a steel wreck. The crew of the submersible piloted the vessel very slowly along the port side close to the rail to the stern of the ship. Almost immediately the cabin came into view. It was completely intact. The wood on the side of the cabin appeared to be inlaid giving the appearance of a picket fence. Then a narrow cabin window appeared with its glass in place and then a second window. In the 1990s, quagga and zebra mussels had not yet taken over the lake so the only covering on the rail and cabin roof was a very thin layer of silt. A cabin companionway provided quick access to the ship's wheel. As the submersible's lights illuminated the wheel, her crew noticed a brass ring around the outside of the wheel. The wheel was in remarkably good condition after decades on the bottom of the lake.

Following an extensive survey of the stern, the SDL-1 moved up along the starboard rail noting the existing deadeyes and belaying pins. At one point on the rail, the crew used the submersible's moveable arm with its grabber to retrieve one of the belaying pins for a sample. Later on in the survey, they also retrieved a sample of the cargo, which was later identified as barley. Moving up to the starboard bow, they observed a lot of damage, which indicated that the bow had hit bottom first. They saw an anchor still hanging in its place. The SDL-1 now moved along the port side past the bow and towards the stern. The foremast was missing but the mainmast still stood. The ropes securing the main boom had rotted away and it had fallen along the middle of the deck. In all, the crew spent over an hour surveying and videoing the wreck site in addition to retrieving several soil samples of the lake bottom near the ship.

When the Canadian Geological Survey released their data, I reviewed my database of over 600 shipwrecks lost in Lake Ontario referencing their survey information. The *Isaac G. Jenkins* is the only ship listed as a two-masted schooner with a length of nearly 140 feet carrying a cargo of barley that sank west of Oswego. I did not participate in the discovery of this wreck but aiding in its identification seemed only natural. A few miles from where the *Jenkins* was reported found is the deepest area of the lake at 805 feet. It's possible that the schooner *Isaac G. Jenkins* is the deepest shipwreck that remains in Lake Ontario.

At the end of November 1875, the schooner *Isaac G. Jenkins* left Milwaukee loaded to capacity with 20,000 bushels of barley, passed through the Welland Canal, heading for Oswego. A fair southwest wind was blowing and which would have delivered the *Jenkins* to its destination within 24 hours. The *Montcalm*, *Nevada*, and *Sam Cook*, three schooners travelling along with her, reported seeing the *Jenkins* off Thirty Mile Point but lost sight of her by nightfall. Early the next morning the schooner was reported seen off the port of Rochester. By then the seas were running high like mountains. This would be the last sighting of the *Isaac G. Jenkins*, the victim of a terrible November gale with 60 miles per hour winds and blinding snow. The next day only a few pieces of floating wreckage from the *Jenkins*, a door and a hatch cover, were found one mile west of Oswego near Sheldon Point. The following day a varnish cask was picked up and a few days later the frozen body of the captain's Newfoundland dog floated into shore. It was reported that of the 10 crew and passengers who perished, at least 8 were Oswegonians. For the next 70 years on the anniversary of its loss, Oswego newspapers published a remembrance of the *Isaac G. Jenkins*.

KNOWN LOST ON THE ISAAC G. JENKINS:

John Brown, Captain — Oswego, New York
Samuel McDonald, First Mate — Oswego, New York
John Smith, Second Mate

Hugh Doran, Seaman — Oswego, New York
William Bonner, Seaman — Oswego, New York
Charles Chetney, Seaman — Oswego, New York
Archie McCullum, Seaman — Oswego, New York
Jennie Williams, Cook — Buffalo, New York
John Stuart, Passenger — Oswego, New York
James Oates, Passenger — Oswego, New York

Note: James Williams and Michael Brophy were originally reported in the Oswego newspapers as being lost on the *Jenkins* but were actually aboard other sailing vessels at the time of the disaster.

The *Isaac G. Jenkins* was built by William Brown in Algonac, Michigan, in 1873. The owners of the *Jenkins* at the time of her loss were Edward and Oliver Mitchell, James Murdoch, and James Dowie.

Isaac G. Jenkins:
US Registration No.: 100178
Vessel Type: schooner
Masts: 2
Decks: 1
Hull Material: wood
Length: 137 ft.
Beam: 25.6 ft.
Depth: 12 ft.
Tonnage: 327 (gross)

SOURCES:

Oswego Daily Palladium, November 29, 1875.
_____, November 30, 1875.
_____, December 1, 1875.
_____, December 2, 1875.
_____, December 3, 1875.

SCHOONER *ATLAS*: SHE SANK LIKE A STONE

Our searches off Oswego begin at 6 a.m. with a two-hour drive to the launch area. Additional time is spent launching our boat and then running out into the lake to our starting point. Generally, we search all day until the sun sets in the west and then return to port. We often grab a quick meal if a restaurant is open before driving home, typically arriving back after 11 p.m. A day searching on the lake can be very boring, watching a featureless bottom on the laptop screen. It definitely helps to have several partners along ready and able to engage in interesting chatter to make the time go by faster. Initially, anticipation is high, as we hope that at any minute an image will appear on computer screen. Sometimes hours go by. Yet, just about the time everyone is nearly dozing off, a significant sonar image might finally appear on the screen. No one is dozing anymore! Such was the day in late June 2013, when a target appeared. Our initial scan of this wreck looked like it was broken up and flattened. The next scan was a much better image and we were pretty sure that we had found the schooner *Atlas*.

In a depth of upwards of 300 feet, the visibility is limited to lighting provided by the ROV. The remains of this wreck can best be described as a mess. This ship sank like the stone we soon learned it was carrying, hitting hard on the bottom of Lake Ontario, which probably collapsed the deck. The impact must have weakened the sides of the schooner causing them to fall away. One of the masts is resting to the starboard side of the wreck and the other is back past the port stern of the ship. Only the aft deck remains with the ship's wheel, heavily encrusted with mussels.

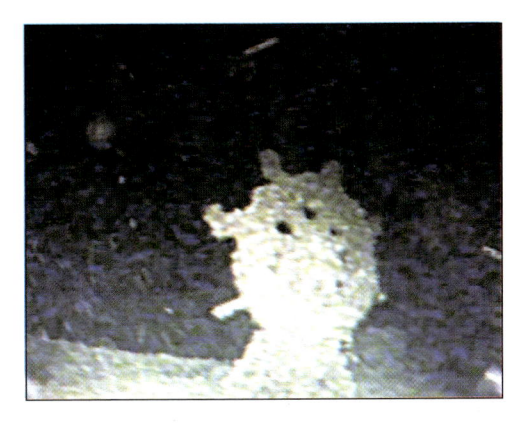

Ship's wheel from the *Atlas*.
Image courtesy of Roger Pawlowski

Just forward of this deck is one of the holds of the ship, containing a large piece of cut stone. From this area to the bow, boards jut out at different angles indicating how violent the impact must have been when it crashed into the bottom. At the bow, one anchor is still hanging on the starboard side while the port anchor is resting on the bottom. The stern of the ship appears to be reinforced — perhaps to support the loading of stone via the stern. The systems aboard the ROV estimated the ship size at 52 feet in length with a beam of 16½ feet. This was only a rough estimate as the wreck was extensively damaged.

The *Atlas* was one of the early commercial schooners to operate on Lake Ontario. She was a two-masted schooner, built in Dexter, New York, in 1838, and owned by Ortha Little & Son. She was built for the specific purpose of transporting building stone from the quarries in the Chaumont, New York area to communities around Lake Ontario. The vessel was small in size with a length of approximately 50 feet and had a cargo carrying capacity of 29 tons. Chaumont is a small town located at the northeastern end of Lake Ontario where there were a number of stone quarries. The blue limestone found in these quarries was classed as superior to all others for use in constructing canals and buildings. The limestone was broken up by driving wedges into

Stone cargo on the *Atlas*.
Image courtesy of Roger Pawlowski

The *Atlas* on lake bottom. Underwater photos (L-R): aft starboard wreckage, deck, starboard bow anchor. Watercolor by Roland E. Stevens III. Images courtesy of Roger Pawlowski

holes drilled in lines along the surface. Once removed, the blocks were usually cut on the ground to the desired shape prior to shipment. From the 1820s to the 1850s, large quantities of limestone were shipped to Oswego for the construction of canal locks, piers, and buildings.

In 1839, Silas Davis won a contract to furnish cut stone for the U.S. government pier in Oswego. On May 4, 1839, the schooner *Atlas* was transporting the Davis' cargo of Black River limestone from Chaumont to the port of Oswego. Within a few miles of its final destination, the *Atlas* encountered gale force winds from the northwest. Several individuals on shore observed the little vessel laboring in the rough seas some miles off. It is more than likely that these turbulent conditions caused the heavy cargo to shift, taking the schooner swiftly to the bottom of Lake Ontario. The schooner sank so quickly no one on board escaped. The *Telegraph* steamed out to the site where the *Atlas* was last seen and recovered a few pieces of flotsam, which included a pair of oars, a coat, two hats, and a pair of boots. A Canadian schooner arriving in Oswego before the *Telegraph* left port reported that it saw no survivors.

Chamount area quarry.   Image courtesy of Town of Lyme

LOST ON THE *ATLAS*

Asahel Westcott, Captain — Brownville, New York
Ortha Little, Part Owner — Hounsfield, New York
William Ackerman, Sailor — Brownville, New York
John See, Sailor
Asa Davis, Brother of Silas Davis (cargo owner) — Chaumont, New York

Stone from the Davis quarries was later used in the construction of the Gerrit Smith building (public library) and a number of other structures in Oswego, many of which still exist today. The lighthouse at the head of Lake Ontario was built from Chaumont stone and some of the market buildings in Kingston, Ontario, made use of the stone from these quarries as well.

Some of the stone quarries are located near Chaumont Bay, which is recessed from Lake Ontario at the eastern end of the lake. Several nearby islands provide additional protection making this location perfect for loading shipments of limestone.

When we found and identified the *Atlas* in 2013, she was the oldest commercial shipwreck discovered in the Great Lakes at that time. Our underwater video survey provided important evidence from a nautical archaeological standpoint as to the construction of an early 19th century Great Lakes vessel. Both the local and national media were excited with the discovery of the *Atlas* and we received some excellent coverage of this shipwreck.

SOURCES:

Oswego County Whig, May 7, 1839.
Oswego Daily Times, January 3, 1891.
Oswego Herald, May 6, 1839.
Oswego Palladium, May 8, 1839.

(A Version of this chapter was published previously in *Inland Seas®*, Summer 2017 — Volume 73)

Ocean Wave: The Schooner That Would Not Sink

Shipwrecks are archaeological sites. On the bottom of the lake, they remain silent until discovered; then, once discovered, the site sometimes reveals its secret history through analysis and interpretation. Often, the site acts like a gateway directing us to other information about the life of the boat prior to the sinking or to the people involved in the boat's operation. This element often humanizes the archaeological site. Nowhere is this more evident than in our discovery in 2012.

That season, we came across a wreck site using the Deepvision side-scan sonar. As is often the case, it took almost a year to get back to the site to survey the remains using the ROV in hopes of identifying the target. Delays such as this one are often caused by weather conditions or timing and prevent us from sending the ROV down immediately. When we sent the ROV to the site, we discovered the full extent of the damage to the shipwreck. Identification of sites that are in major disrepair, such as this one, is often difficult but we believed enough of the hull of this shipwreck was intact to provide a solid length measurement. Much of deck, much of the stern and the cabin are missing. The masts are gone except for a three-to-four-foot stub of the foremast. Both sides of the ship have fallen away and lay open next to the hull. Except for the area around the bow, most of the vessel lies flat as a pancake on the bottom. The anchors that would have hung on the bow rail and the windlass used to hoist them are missing.

Side-scan sonar image of *Ocean Wave*.
Image courtesy of Jim Kennard

After reviewing the video survey, we struggled to explain the condition of this wreck site. Was the damage to the vessel caused by the impact with the lake bottom? Even in freshwater, wrecks will deteriorate "naturally."

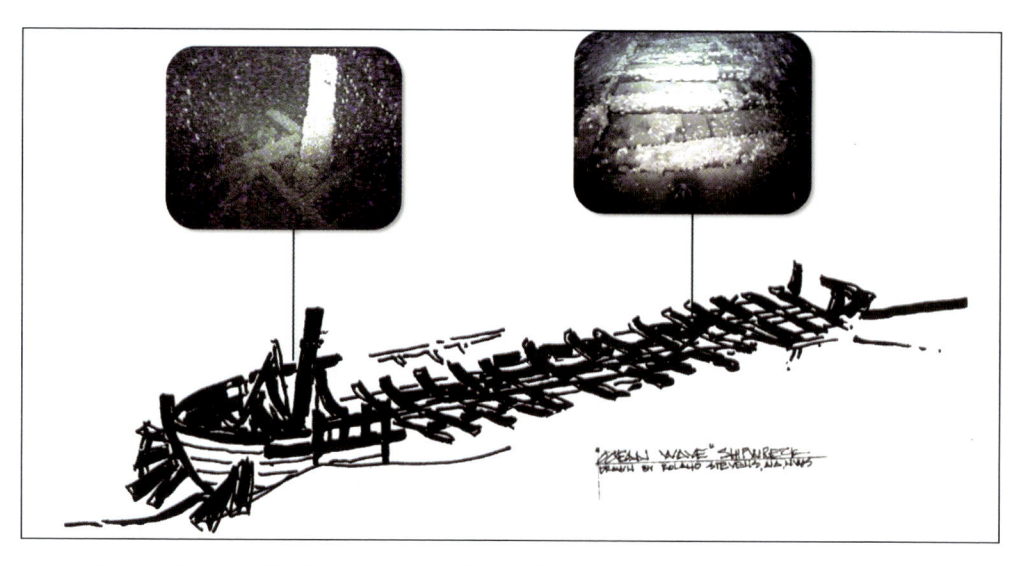

Ocean Wave underwater. Underwater photos (L-R): foremast remains, frames.
Drawing by Roland E. Stevens III. Images courtesy of Roger Pawlowski

Wrecks in shallow waters, particularly in the waters of Lake Erie, are often destroyed over time by the impact of wave action and even the movement of ice during the winter. But this wreck site was in deep water. Or, did its current condition hold some secret as to its identity? To narrow the list of potential candidates we followed the process that has worked so well for us for so many years. The ROV sector-scanning sonar system estimated the length of the vessel at approximately 80 feet. We reviewed lists of vessel losses, looking for two-masted vessels of that length that sank midway between Oswego and Mexico Bay. We narrowed the field of candidates and hypothesized that this wreck might be the *Ocean Wave*. In the story of her loss, we found evidence that explains the condition of the wreck as it sits on the bottom of the lake.

The *Ocean Wave*, a two-masted schooner, was built in Picton, Ontario, in 1868, and was owned by Captains Thomas Brokenshire and William Martin, both of Port Hope. The schooner was 81 feet long, with a beam of 20 feet, and a carrying capacity of nearly 100 tons, or 100,000 feet of lumber. On November 11, 1890, the schooner was heavily laden with a cargo of hemlock lumber and lath, bound for Oswego from Trenton, Ontario. The cargo belonged to George McChesney of Syracuse and William McChesney of Oswego. When the

Captain Thomas Brokenshire.
Image courtesy of Richard Nereau

schooner was within 15 miles of Oswego, it encountered a sudden and violent squall from the south. At the same time, a tugboat captain towing five barges approximately 30 miles to the northeast was forced to run with his tow to the port of Cape Vincent in the St. Lawrence River. He commented on the intensity of the storm. "It lashed the lake into a raging torrent that no vessel could have lived through." The winds at Oswego were recorded as high as 34 mph, however, based on my experience and research, in the middle of the lake, the winds could have been over 45 mph. The waves created by these high winds may have exceeded 12 feet in height.

The following day there were several reports from ships coming into port that they had passed what appeared to be the schooner *Ocean Wave* now bottom up and floating in the lake. A section of the stern with its cargo of lath was reported floating northward. A tugboat was sent out from Oswego to rescue any survivors and possibly retrieve the sinking ship. The tugboat described the stricken vessel as on its port side with just a portion of the starboard rail above the water with her spars floating nearby. The stern had been washed away and only a small portion of the lumber cargo remained in the hold. The yawl was still attached to the schooner. No survivors were found. The squall must have come very fast and hit hard, not giving the crew any time to reach the yawl and possible safety. Because the *Ocean Wave* was so badly broken up and the cargo of lumber nearly gone, the vessel was not considered worth towing back to Oswego.

After the squall, the winds subsided for the next week and the *Ocean Wave* continued to float around Lake Ontario at the mercy of the wind and lake currents often becoming a hazard to passing ships. Ten days later, some of the debris from the schooner reached Mexico Bay at the eastern end of Lake Ontario. However, the hull of the *Ocean Wave* was not with this flotsam. The ship had finally sank somewhere along the way.

The wife of Captain Brokenshire reported to the *Daily British Whig* of Kingston that there were five persons on the *Ocean Wave*; her husband Captain Brokenshire and William Martin of Port Hope; Mr. Smith of Port Hope; Mr. Joseph Wells of Belleville, and an unknown man. The unknown man was later to be revealed as Tommy Sands of Port Hope, about 18 years old and an immigrant. Captain Brokenshire left 12 children, four of whom were still at home, the oldest being 12 and the youngest 4 years old.

Richard Nereau is the great grandson of Captain Brokenshire and currently lives in Geneseo near Rochester. Some years ago Richard received a letter from one of his Canadian relatives that provided additional details of the captain's family and the events just prior to the departure of the *Ocean Wave* on its final voyage.

The late Captain Nelson Palmatier, veteran mariner of Cherry Valley, was probably the last person ashore to see and talk to Captain Brokenshire. Captain Palmatier was in Trenton at the time that the *Ocean Wave* was being loaded to the hatches with lumber for Oswego. He borrowed the yawl boat and upon returning remarked that it was leaking and needed repairs. Captain Brokenshire replied that "she will do our turn, this is the last trip we are going to make. We have good freight on this lumber and we'll pick up a load of coal in Oswego and go home with it to Cobourg and settle down ashore for the rest of our lives.

Family letter detailing events related to the loss of the *Ocean Wave*.
Image courtesy of Richard Nereau

(L-R) Roland Stevens, Jim Kennard, Margaret Nereau, Richard Nereau, and Roger Pawlowski. Image courtesy of Marilyn Kennard

The Brokenshires had a number of relatives living in the Rochester, New York area. The wife of Captain Brokenshire eventually moved there, as did two of his daughters — Faney and Catherine — all settling in East Rochester. They are buried in a nearby cemetery in Penfield, New York. Catherine was the youngest of the Brokenshire's children and was the grandmother of Mr. Nereau.

Maritime history is replete with references to the victims of shipwrecks that were thought to be on the last trip of the season, or the last trip of their career. I am not sure if this phenomenon is more often urban legend, as opposed to fact. But in the case of the *Ocean Wave*, the letter provides a haunting but human face to the possibility that on the last trip of his career, Captain Brokenshire's luck ran out and he became a victim of the lake that had sustained him for so many years. What is equally haunting is that Captain Brokenshire, two years before, had saved the crew of the *William Elgin*, as that boat sank to the depths of Lake Ontario. This hero of the *Elgin* disaster had no one nearby to save him and his crew in the sudden storm in November 1890.

SOURCES:

Oswego Daily Times, November 17, 1890.
_____, November 22, 1890.
Oswego Daily Palladium, November 16, 1890.
Robinson, Muriel. Letter to Richard Nereau. Private Collection.

(A Version of this chapter was published previously in *Inland Seas®,* Summer 2017 — Volume 73)

CANADIAN STEAMER *ROBERVAL*

Roberval circa 1907.   Photo courtesy of Jim Kennard

In late summer 2012, our shipwreck search team concluded our shipwreck search efforts off Sodus Point and headed up to Oswego to look for the steamer *Roberval* but with no success. The next year, we returned to that area and were fortunate to make several discoveries; the schooners *Atlas*, lost in 1839, the *Ocean Wave*, lost in 1890, and the *Black Duck*, which sank in 1872 (detailed in a later chapter) — but still no *Roberval*. We continued to search off Oswego during the 2013 season and explored 90 square miles of the lake bottom in an effort to find this long-sought shipwreck; we came up empty handed time and time again. By mid-October, the marinas were closing for the season and very few boaters were on the lake. On our last day of the 2013 shipwreck search season, with calm waters and light winds, we decided to do a "Hail Mary" search and ventured farther out on the lake than ever before to start a new search pattern. Within 90 minutes we were rewarded with the discovery of a shipwreck. The remainder of the day was spent surveying the wreck to obtain detailed sonar imagery with a high-resolution side-scan sonar followed up by video obtained from the ROV.

Was this the *Roberval* lost in 1916 while carrying a deck load of lumber?

Watching the video feed from the ROV, we confirmed the initial side-scan sonar image that suggested the wreck experienced incredible physical destruction. Gone are the cabins and much of the ship's decking. A portion of the starboard side of the ship toward the stern has collapsed and fallen away, despite this clearly being a steel hull. At the bow, some of the raised deck still exists with a large windlass present. Behind it is a smaller windlass, which was used to raise and lower a boom attached to a mast located just forward of mid-ship. The mast is broken and part of it extends over the port rail. The port side of the steamer is buried within a few feet of its deck. Remains of iron posts that were part of the railing are clearly visible in the sonar imagery and portions of the video. Unlike many of the early 19th century shipwrecks we have discovered, there are photographs of the *Roberval* that can aid in shipwreck identification. With historic photographs of the *Roberval*, we closely compared the video of the iron posts hoping for a match. A small portion of the deck at the rounded stern is visible along with what appears to be two square bollards still in place, one behind the other. Around the periphery of the wreck are other pieces of ship debris. Our measuring capabilities onboard the ROV and the side-scan confirmed that this wreck was approximately 128 feet in length and has about a 24-foot beam. Since only two steel steamers sank in Lake Ontario over the years, and only one in the eastern portion of the lake, we were able to identify this steel steamer as our long-sought *Roberval*.[1] The absence of any of her lumber cargo on the deck was also telling. The story of her loss helped explain the frightening damage that befell her.

The steel steamer *Roberval* was built by the Polson Iron Works in Toronto, Ontario, in 1907, and owned by Captains Eligh and Hall of

Side-scan sonar image of *Roberval*.
Image courtesy of Jim Kennard

---

[1] The other steel steamship *Nesbit Grammer* was thought to have been lost in the western portion in Lake Ontario.

Roberval Underwater. Underwater photos (L-R): bow showing damage, midships.
Watercolor by Roland E. Stevens III. Images courtesy of Roger Pawlowski

Ottawa. The steamer had a registered length of 128 feet, a beam of 24 feet, and a capacity of 344 gross tons. The *Roberval* was known as one of the best built steel boats on Lake Ontario at the time. She had been built for the saltwater trade, but by 1916, she had been on Lake Ontario for years carrying lumber from Ottawa to Oswego, returning to Canada with coal.

On September 25, 1916, the *Roberval* carried a huge load of spruce lumber, 248,000 board feet, destined to be made into boxes for matchsticks by the Diamond Match Company in Oswego. The steamer departed Cape Vincent on the banks of the St. Lawrence River in the early afternoon and within an hour was on Lake Ontario heading south to its destination. As the afternoon progressed, northwest winds on the lake increased to over 30 miles per hour. These winds were not typically excessive for this ship, but the large stack of lumber piled on deck acted as a sail catching the wind, which made it very difficult for the steamer to stay on course. As the winds increased so did the waves, reaching heights of over eight feet, which continually hit the *Roberval,* rolling her from side to side. Eventually, several waves combined into one huge "rogue" wave causing the steamer to roll over on its starboard side spilling a portion of the deck cargo. This was followed by another large wave, which caused the remaining cargo to slide off the deck and into the cabin at the aft portion of the steamer.

Apparently, everything happened so fast there was little time to comprehend the extent of the danger. The waves smashed the galley window and flooded the gangway. The upper structure of the cabin area was bashed in and one of the lifeboats was destroyed. As water filled the engine room, the stern slowly sank. Four of the crew attempted to man the remaining lifeboat, when suddenly the *Roberval* took another wave throwing three men into the water and Chief Engineer Phillip Trottier into the lifeboat. First Fireman Marcel Messenau opted to stay with the pile of floating lumber while the other two men climbed into the now-damaged second lifeboat. The second fireman, Henry Seguin, who had been down in the firehole, managed to reach the deck just as the ship plunged under. While he stood on the port side bewildered, a pile of sliding timber struck him in the back and head knocking him into the lake where he drowned. Members of the crew reported they could see Seguin's lifeless body about five feet below the surface of the water as they started to pull away from the wreck.

The cook, Miss Delia Parent, was hanging on for dear life at the bow rail. Captain Peter Eligh brought her aft where he told her to hang on to the iron railing running around the cabin structure. However, as the stern of the ship sank deeper into the water, she was thrown over the starboard side into the lake. Following her, the captain grasped several timbers, slid down the deck and then leaped, landing in the water within a few feet of where the cook had sunk several feet underwater. He grabbed her by the hair and dragged her to a nearby timber for support. A short distance away, the first mate was struggling to get enough lumber to make a raft. The spruce timbers the vessel was carrying were not large in size, only one to six inches in width and 8 to 13 feet in length. The conditions of the lake at that time, as well as the size of the timbers in the water, made it nearly impossible for members of the crew to construct emergency life rafts. But they did!

In the forward deckhouse of the sinking ship, which was now nearly vertical in the water, above those constructing the raft, appeared the young deckhand, Theodore Leroy, in one of the porthole windows. The roar of the wind and the crash of the waves were so loud they could not hear his pleas for help. The unfortunate young man was trapped by falling lumber that had blocked the exit. He would eventually go down with the ship. The three men in the lifeboat could see the others clinging to the mass of floating timbers which covered the lake in all directions. They made several attempts at rescue, but were buffeted about by the waves and were unable to reach their companions. As darkness fell, the men in the lifeboat had to abandon their attempts at rescue and focus on reaching the safety of shore many miles away.

Around 5:30 p.m., the *Roberval* lost its deck load and began to slowly sink below the surface of Lake Ontario. It was temporarily stopped in a near vertical position by the floatation provided by 150,000 board feet of dry spruce lumber in the hold of the steamer. The *Glen Allen*, a sister ship that was seven miles behind the *Roberval* at the time of the accident, saw what they thought was the sun reflecting off the deck lumber. In fact, it might have been a reflection of the sun off the vertical wet hull that was now protruding high out of the water.

The bow of the lifeboat occupied by three of the crew had been severely damaged and was leaking badly. The three men in this small craft bailed water and rowed for nearly nine hours to the port of Oswego, a distance of over 16 miles. The *Glen Allen* had arrived in port at 8:30 p.m. and soon afterwards Captain Clark went over to the Coast Guard station to check on the arrival of the *Roberval*, but there was no report of the ship. He thought that perhaps the *Roberval* had ridden out the storm on the open lake. The three survivors in the lifeboat arrived in Oswego at 2 a.m. and went straight to the Coast Guard station to alert them of the *Roberval* disaster and that four crewmembers were last seen alive and floating on the deck load of lumber now in the water. The Coast Guard immediately launched their power boat and headed off towards the location where the survivors thought the *Roberval* had foundered.

Meanwhile Captain Eligh, First Mate Parisien, and the cook Miss Parent, were struggling to keep the timbers together. As darkness fell, the lake current slowly carried them away from the *Roberval*, which was still floating with its bow section visible just above the water. The captain and Miss Parent both had found life preservers among the floating debris. One of the life preservers was equipped with an automatic beacon light, which could be activated by pulling several small rings on its side. Captain Eligh repeatedly tried to activate the beacon, but it just would not work. Frustrated by his many futile attempts, he threw the beacon out into the lake where — upon impact — it turned on. For the next few hours they watched it glowing brightly as it floated away with the current. All night long the three were hammered by the waves but miraculously held their makeshift raft together. At daybreak, the lake settled down and in the distance, about half a mile away, they could see Messenau, the first fireman, who had decided to take his chances with the floating debris instead of the damaged lifeboat. He had attempted to put together a raft of timbers but could not keep them together due to the turbulence on the lake. Finally, he spied a water cask and abandoned the timbers for this new floating raft. As the waves calmed, he left the water cask and created a new raft. Messenau soon was able to join his shipmates and they combined their rafts to fortify the floating platform of timbers.

As the sun rose and illuminated the land, the crew of now four on the makeshift raft realized that they were drifting in the vicinity of Mexico Bay. The shifting winds had sent the imperiled crew and floating debris field away from the main course used by other commercial vessels. The captain must have known the implication of their current position on the effort to locate them. For nearly a day, the Coast Guard from both Oswego and the Big Sandy Stations searched for survivors of the *Roberval*. Unfortunately, the lifesavers were not searching far enough from Oswego to find the castaways. By mid-afternoon on September 26, the four castaways had been on the raft for over 22 hours. Nightfall was only a few hours away. Without rescue, hypothermia and death were sure to follow as the temperature of the water in late September was growing colder.

Seeing victims collapsed on a flat makeshift raft from the Big Sandy Coast Guard vessel which also rode low in the water, was almost an impossible task. Finally, one of the Coast Guard crew sighted a large flock of birds resting on some debris in the lake. A number of birds could be seen hovering and then flying away from that location. The Coast Guard boat headed to the area to check it out and found the survivors of the *Roberval* alive. Several hours later, the four arrived at the Big Sandy Coast Guard station for treatment. The men were released but Miss Parent remained for some medical attention. Fortunately none of them had suffered any serious effects due to exposure. By the next day, the deck load of lumber could be found scattered along the east shore of Lake Ontario all the way to the St. Lawrence River.

CREW OF THE STEAMER *ROBERVAL*

Survived:
Peter Eligh, Captain — Ottawa, Ontario
Joseph Parisien, First Mate — Alfred, Ontario
Philip Trottier, Chief Engineer — Hull, Quebec
Oliver Sequin, Second Engineer — Hull, Quebec
Marcel Messenau, First Fireman — Hull, Quebec
Miss Delia Parent, Cook — Ottawa, Ontario
Edward Legault, Wheelsman — St. Anne Bellevue, Quebec

Drowned
Henry Seguin, Second Fireman — Hull, Quebec
Theodore Leroy, Deckhand — Hull, Quebec

Photo of Captain Peter Eligh's family.   Image courtesy of Jim Kennard

When someone survives a shipwreck, there is a firsthand account of what happened. When we began looking for the *Roberval* years ago, we knew her story and in many ways, that story motivated us to look for, and eventually discover, this important shipwreck. It took us five seasons to find the *Roberval* but it was worth the wait. Yet, I never tire of rereading the account of her survivors, which had served to motivate us for so many years.

SOURCES:

Oswego Daily Palladium, September 26, 1916.
_____, September 27, 1916.
_____, September 28, 1916.

ABOVE AND BELOW LAKE ONTARIO: USAF C-45

There are more than shipwrecks lying on the bottom of Lake Ontario. In the past 110 years, several commercial and military aircraft have ended up in the lake. Most notable is an X-2 high-speed experimental aircraft that exploded in October 1953 over Lake Ontario. Other military aircraft, including a B-24, C-47, and C-45, also made their final landings at the bottom of the lake.

In 1980, my dive partner, Scott Hill, and I located a Cessna 172 aircraft that ran out of fuel before it could make it to land. My more recent shipwreck exploration teammate, Roger Pawlowski, had hoped that we would locate one of those military aircraft mentioned above. In 1956, as a young lad of eight, he became fascinated with airplanes. Living in Tonawanda, New York, he would pack a lunch, put it in the large basket on the front of his bike, and pedal seven miles to the Niagara Falls airport. He had a favorite spot where he would camp out for the day and watch the airplanes take off and land. One day a pilot for a Niagara Falls tour flight spotted him and asked Roger if he was interested in a ride. "How much?" Roger asked. "Five dollars," the pilot replied. "I only have three dollars," said Roger. "That will do," said the pilot. The pilot was operating a Beach 18, the commercial version of the military C-45 aircraft, and Roger got to sit in the co-pilot seat. Multiple trips to the airport that summer fostered a passion for building models of various airplanes, including the Beach 18. Later, in college he enrolled in ROTC where one of his instructors took him flying in a T-33 jet trainer. Roger eventually earned the opportunity to fly the T-33. Roger's passion and hard work paid off as he was nominated and given the Lawrence D. Bell Award as the most promising pilot candidate in ROTC. After graduating from the University of Buffalo, he joined the U.S. Air Force spending time at the Vance Air Force Base in Enid, Oklahoma. There Roger learned to fly the big cargo carrying C-130 aircraft, which he would continue to do for the next 25 years in the Air Force Reserve. He is a veteran of the 1989–1990 Desert Storm conflict where he flew C-130s into Iraq and also landed in the jungles of Columbia. He never lost an aircraft.

In June 2014, Roger, Chip, and I located an aircraft while surveying the lake bottom off Oswego, New York. Searching the Oswego area had been very fruitful over the past years but our discoveries had all been vessel related. We were surprised when an image of an aircraft appeared on our sonar display, as the C-45 we hoped to find was thought to be well beyond a mile offshore, as reported in 1952 by a few eyewitnesses. However, we have found over the years that the quality of eyewitness reporting of marine disasters is often weak, particularly when reporting a location on open water. Regardless, our excitement immediately rose to new heights because if we had found the C-45 lost in 1952, we had found the same type of aircraft that Roger had taken his first plane ride in when he was eight years old.

We spent the next few hours obtaining detailed sonar images of the aircraft wreck by utilizing the side- scan sonar. When we take detailed sonar images, it allows us to understand how the wreckage lies on the bottom of the lake. The sonar search was followed up by deploying the ROV to collect video of the wreck site. When the ROV landed near the aircraft, the amount of natural light and the lack of particulate in the water created ideal conditions for videography. Roger quickly confirmed that we had found the lost United States Air Force C-45 aircraft. Except for a few pieces, we were amazed to see an almost totally intact plane. The fiberglass nose cone is missing, as are the vertical stabilizers. One of the blades of the left propeller is broken off and lies nearby on the lake bottom. Part of the windshield is broken and the left side of the body behind the wing has been torn away. Otherwise it is all there. This probably explains why no debris was ever found floating on the surface of the lake during the searches conducted by the US Coast Guard and US Air Force. For our team member and retired Air Force Reserve pilot, Lt. Col. Pawlowski, it was a very special discovery.

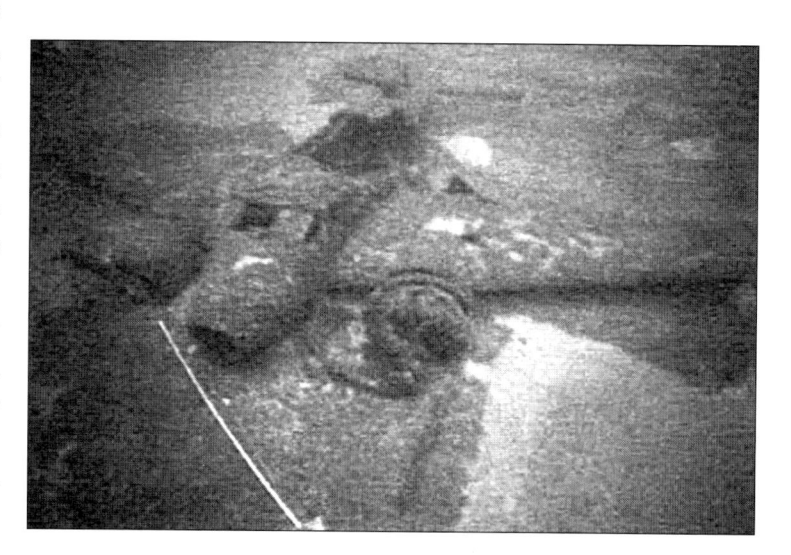

C-45. Image courtesy of Roger Pawlowski

On September 10, 1952, a United States Air Force C-45 aircraft took off from Bedford, Massachusetts, on a routine flight to Griffiss Air Force Base near Rome, New York. The C-45 was used by the military as a staff and utility transport plane with seating for six to eight people. When the flight was

C-45. Image courtesy of Roger Pawlowski

40 miles southeast of Utica, the left engine began to fail. The aircraft started to lose altitude about eight miles from Rome, New York. Believing the plane would crash after the one engine failed, the pilot, Lt. Col. Charles Callahan, ordered his crew and passengers to open the door and jettison everything they could to lighten the load — but the C-45 continued to lose altitude. Lt. Col. Callahan then looked for a suitable place to land but was unable to identify one. As the plane continued to lose altitude, Lt. Col. Callahan surmised that the plane would soon reach an altitude too low to make a safe jump. Callahan ordered everyone out. Three Air Force officers and two civilians made the first parachute jump of their lives from an altitude of only 2,500 feet. Miraculously they all landed safely.

Prior to leaving the aircraft, Callahan set the automatic pilot on a heading northwest which he believed would take it clear of any inhabited area. The aircraft, which had been heading towards the ground, was now lighter by nearly 1,000 pounds and suddenly gained altitude. At this increased height, and with a new direction, the C-45 flew northwest towards the city of Oswego for the next hour and 10 minutes until its fuel ran out. At 11 p.m., reports indicated that the aircraft was flying very low over a residential area west of Oswego, New York. The owner of Rudy's refreshment stand and his employee saw a plane fly overhead just before it plunged into the water. They both reported that, "a powerful light, like that of a searchlight, appeared for several seconds after the crash."

C-45. Image courtesy of Roger Pawlowski

The search for the missing plane began immediately by three US Coast Guard cutters. In addition, a variety of military plans such as C-45 trainers, C-47 transports, and B-25 bombers combed the crash area for 24 hours.

Rudy's. Drawing by Roland E. Stevens III

When there was no wreckage found and when searchers realized that all the individuals from the abandoned C-45 had actually parachuted and landed safely, the search was called off.

CREW OF USAF C-45

Lt. Col. Charles A. Callahan, Pilot — Monticello, Mississippi
Lt. Sam Sharff — New York City, New York
Lt. Col. G. S. Lambert — Newport News, Virginia
William P. Bethke, Civilian Technician — near Rome, New York
Joseph M. Eannario, Civilian Observer — Rome, New York

Charles Callahan.
Image courtesy of Patrick D. Callahan

USAF C-45. Image courtesy of Larry Westin

U.S. AIR FORCE C-45 SPECIFICATIONS

Wingspan: 47 ft. 8 in.
Length: 34 ft. 3 in.
Height: 9 ft. 8 in.
Manufacturer: Beach Aircraft Corporation
Engines: Pratt & Whitney R986 AN 1 Wasp Junior 9-cylinder radial air cooled — 450 HP
Speed (maximum): 215 mph
Ceiling Height (maximum): 20,000 ft.
Loaded weight: 8727 lbs.
Range: 700 miles
Manned by two men and carried 6 to 8 passengers with no armament.

Solving an historical mystery is one of great rewards of discovering and identifying a shipwreck. In this case, it pales in comparison to the satisfaction I felt seeing Roger help find Lake Ontario's only C-45 plane wreck. Yet, one week after we announced our discovery, I received an email from the nephew of Lt. Col. Charles A. Callahan. He related some of the details of the abandoned flight as described above prior to the crew jumping out of the aircraft. In addition, he mentioned that it was a family joke that Uncle Charles "had a well-deserved reputation for having wrecked and walked away from more airplanes than anyone else in the Air Force…." Sometimes, when finding a shipwreck, the rewards come in sets of two.

REFERENCES:

Callahan, Patrick. Electronic message to author. July 14, 2014.
Oswego Palladium Times, September 11, 1952.
_____, September 12, 1952.
_____, September 13, 1952.

(A Version of this chapter was published previously in *Inland Seas*®, Summer 2017 — Volume 73)

ANOTHER DAGGERBOARD: *THREE BROTHERS*

Three Brothers under sail. Watercolor by Roland E. Stevens III

In early July 2014, the shipwreck search team consisting of Roger, Roland, and I were searching in a deep area of Lake Ontario west of Oswego, New York, utilizing high-resolution side-scan sonar. The discovery of a schooner came as a complete surprise since this was not one of the shipwrecks thought to be in this area. After making several passes with the side-scan sonar around the shipwreck, we studied the images to determine the characteristics of the ship. Something looked very familiar in the sonar shadow cast by the profile of the sunken ship. It appeared to be a long continuous partition in the mid-section of this schooner. As we prepared the remote operated vehicle for deployment to explore the wreck the excitement was high in anticipation of confirming that this new discovery might be another rare daggerboard schooner.

When we deployed the ROV, the natural lighting was perfect for illuminating the shipwreck and the entire wreck was captured in the video image.

Almost immediately we saw that this shipwreck was very special. A large single daggerboard rises up from the center of the shipwreck. The daggerboard on this vessel measures 12 feet in length and protrudes 4 feet above the deck. The overall length of the shipwreck is approximately 45 feet with a width of 13 feet. There are two large holds on either side of the daggerboard. On the second dive, the ROV descended into each hold to look for any remaining cargo. Each appears empty except for a layer of sediment and the top of a barrel. The schooner does not have a raised cabin but only a companionway that leads to a small area below deck near the stern of the ship. Scattered remains of boards and pottery can be seen in this area.

Side-scan sonar image of the *Three Brothers*. Image courtesy of Jim Kennard

The masts had been torn from the ship when it sank and lay nearby along with some of the decking that was also pulled away. A single anchor remains fastened in place next to the windlass. There are many holes in the

Three Brothers underwater. Underwater photos (L-R): bow to midship, stern cabin hatchway, stern and rudder. Watercolor by Roland E. Stevens III. Images courtesy of Roger Pawlowski

deck caused by wood rot. The ship was steered by a tiller, which is missing. Upon impact with the lake bottom, the rudder probably dislodged from the stern and much of it is buried into the lake bottom.

For six weeks we investigated possible identities that might match the conditions of this shipwreck. We collaborated with shipwreck historians seeking any clues to help identify this schooner. A friend and fellow researcher, Dennis McCarthy, suggested that this wreck might be the schooner *Three Brothers*, identified from a transcript of remembrances by Captain James Van Cleve. Provided with a name, we located additional research material including several articles in the Oswego newspapers that helped to confirm the identity of the schooner *Three Brothers*.

Galloo Island is located a few miles from the northeastern end of Lake Ontario near the St. Lawrence River. Several schooners and scows were built on Galloo, including the schooner *Three Brothers*, built by Whitford Gill in 1827. Gill was the first longterm resident to settle on Galloo. He purchased land at the foot of the island in 1815, and in 1822, brought his family to live there where he tended two orchards and operated a saw mill. In addition to the *Three Brothers*, Gill built two other schooners, *Old Taylor* and *Galloo*.

The schooner *Three Brothers* was owned by Asahel and Bethel Todd of Pultneyville and Captain Stevenson of Williamson, New York. On the morning of November 12, 1833, the schooner *Three Brothers* sailed from Pultneyville to Oswego, New York, with a cargo of apples, cider, and 700 bushels of wheat. Unfortunately the schooner failed to arrive at Oswego. People suspected that the *Three Brothers* foundered in the gale that blew that day. Within a few days of the gale, the ship's tiller, a barrel of apples, and the captain's hat were found just east of Oswego near Nine Mile Point.

PERSONS LOST ON THE *THREE BROTHERS*

John Stevenson, Captain — Willliamson, New York
Cephas Field, Crewmember — Sodus, New York
William Bastian, Crewmember — Mexico, New York
Amos Gloyed, Passenger — French Creek, New York

A plaque in the center of Pultneyville, New York, dedicated to the memory of lake captains of Pultneyville, lists Captain John Stevenson of the *Three Brothers*, 1833.

The discovery of the *Three Brothers* provided very good details of a nearly intact daggerboard schooner, one of the Great Lakes very rare ships.

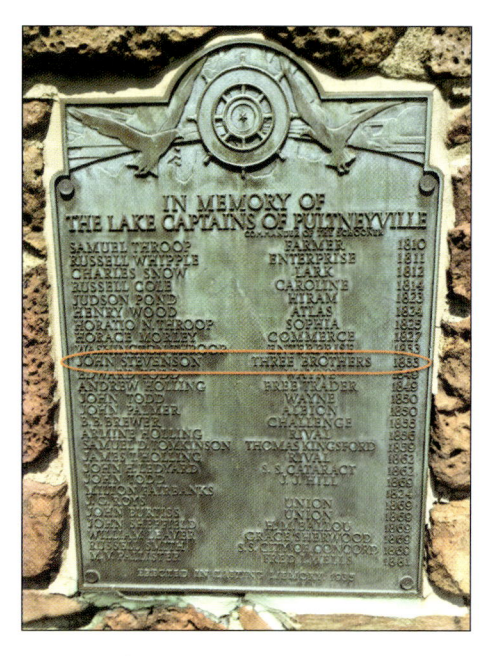

Pultneyville, New York plaque dedicated to lost captains.
Image courtesy of Teddy Garlock

REFERENCES:

Oswego Free Press, December 4, 1833.

Oswego Palladium, November 20, 1833.

Three Brothers. Enrollment Documents, 1827-1833.

Van Cleve, James. "Reminiscences of Early Steamboats, Propellers and Sailing Vessels on Lake Ontario and River St. Lawrence." Unpublished manuscript, 1877.

Wayne Sentinel [Palmyra, New York], November 29, 1833.

STEAMSHIP *NISBET GRAMMER*: LAKE ONTARIO'S LARGEST SHIPWRECK

Nisbet Grammer.   Image courtesy of Bascom Collection

In September 2008, Dan Scoville and I began our initial search for the largest steel steamer ever to sink in Lake Ontario, the *Nisbet Grammer*. We thought the wreck would be easy to find since the Canadian Marine Court of Inquiry's final report provided excellent information about the ship and its collision with the *Dalwarnic*, but the map associated with the report was missing. Our search turned out to be more of a challenge than expected. During the next six years, we surveyed more than 80 square miles of deep lake bottom looking for the *Grammer* without success.

In late August 2014, Dan, Roland, Craig Hampton, and I found the *Grammer* midway between Niagara and Rochester, New York. Craig is an old friend from Lake Erie who decided to come east that summer to help out. On this search, we utilized an Imagenex Yellow Fin side-scan sonar system towed by a 2,000 foot steel cable controlled by a specially constructed winch designed by Dan. Craig's boat featured an autopilot, which provided accurate coverage of the targeted search area. The search grid was determined by researching the Court of Inquiry documents. Then, over the years, we expanded the area. Though we spent many years looking for the

Grammer without success, we did discover, in that same area of the lake, the unidentified rare daggerboard schooner detailed in an earlier chapter.

Having already discovered the only other historic steel steamship shipwreck in Lake Ontario, the *Roberval*, we were fairly confident that we found her simply based on her measurements. The side-scan sonar gave us an initial length measurement of about 250 feet. Even though we were sure this was the *Grammer*, we were not about to give up the chance to explore this gem with Dan's ROV. The ROV designed by Dan uses a special thin fiber optic tether to communicate with the topside electronics and video display. Use of a thin tether has the distinct advantage of minimizing the drag caused by lake currents when deploying very long lengths of cable to reach the deep depths of Lake Ontario. Over 900 feet of fiber optic tether was used to reach this shipwreck, which lies at a depth of over 500 feet!

There were very strong lake currents on the day the team surveyed the steamship with the ROV. It was literally a tug of war as Dan fought the effect of the lake currents on the long tether to eventually inch the ROV to the hull of the *Nisbet Grammer*. Arriving at the base of the starboard bow of the large steamer, the hull appeared as a great wall just waiting to be conquered. The ROV ascended approximately 40 feet to the bow rail. Peering through the railing, we could see the staircase leading up to the pilothouse. This glimpse of the big steamer was all that we saw because one of the ROV thrusters failed, preventing any forward movement. Sadly the mission to explore the remaining details of *Nisbet Grammer* would have to wait for another time.

In the early 1920s, large steamships carrying grain from the Upper Lakes had to be unloaded at either Port Colborne or Buffalo onto smaller vessels to pass through the Welland Canal in order to reach eastern coastal ports. In December 1922, seven individuals connected with the grain business formed the Eastern Steamship Company Ltd. of St. Catharines, Ontario. They commissioned the construction of ten canallers, which would be able to transport grain across the Upper Lakes and also pass through the canal from Lake Erie to Lake Ontario. G. J. Grammer and his son Nisbet Grammer were two of the founders of the new steamship company. Nisbet was also the president of the Eastern Grain, Mill & Elevator Corporation of Buffalo. He was subsequently elected president of the Eastern Steamship Company.

The *Nisbet Grammer* was built in the shipyard of Cammell Laird and Company of Birkenhead, England, and on April 14, 1923, the canaller was launched into the Mersey River. Like ship launchings everywhere, this event was attended by thousands who interpreted the sun coming out from

> **NISBET GRAMMER SPECIFICATIONS**
>
> Length: 253 feet
> Beam: 43.1 feet
> Depth: 17.9 feet
> Gross Tonnage: 1725
> Net Tonnage: 1110
> Hold Capacity: 130,000 cubic feet
> Mean Draft loaded: 14 feet
> Engine: Surface-condensing inverted triple-expansion steam engine
> Maximum Speed: 10 knots
> The engines were coal-fired fed from wing bunkers.
> Two large single-ended Scotch boilers (Diameter: 12 ft. x length: 11 ft.) provided a steam pressure of 180 pound per square inch to run the engines.

behind the clouds just as the *Grammer* slid down the ways as a favorable sign for things to come. This was not to be.

In the early morning hours of May 31, 1926, the *Nisbet Grammer* took on a load of grain at Buffalo then passed through the Welland Canal into Lake Ontario destined for Montreal down the St. Lawrence River. The lake was calm with a slight wind from the northeast. Around 4:30 a.m., a dense fog formed limiting visibility to several hundred feet. The *Grammer* could only hear the warning sounds of another ship's fog horn as it passed in the night. The steamer continued on but reduced its speed in half (to four-and-a-half knots) for the next hour. As time passed, the fog grew thicker. At 5:30 a.m., the sound of a new fog horn was heard, almost directly in their path. Within just a few minutes, the Canadian steamship *Dalwarnic* appeared. The *Grammer* immediately turned to starboard to avoid the oncoming steamer but there was not enough time for the 253-foot steamship to avoid the fatal collision. The *Dalwarnic* struck the *Grammer* on the port side near the stern just forward of the boilerhouse and engine compartment. A lifeboat from the *Nisbet Grammer* was deployed, as was a yawl from the *Dalwarnic*, which allowed the crew to safely escape from the sinking steamship. In less than 15 minutes, the *Nisbet Grammer*'s hull filled with water and sank stern first into the depths of Lake Ontario.

A formal investigation into the circumstances of the collision and sinking was held in Toronto on June 15–17, 1926. The 258-page court transcript

The Collision.   Watercolor by Roland E. Stevens III

provided a detailed account of both vessels leading up to accident. This document included the speeds, mileage, and times as stated by both ships' captains. We used this information to narrow down the probable search area for the wreck. Due to the poor visibility created by the dense fog, both sides made mistakes. As a result of the inquiry, "the certificate of the *Nisbet Grammer* captain, A. Laking, was suspended for failing to give specific instructions to his officer. The first mate, M. Robson, was suspended for three months for not having stopped the ship, sounded the alarm signals, or awakened and alerted the captain. The certificate of the captain of the *Dalwarnic*, J. A. Cuthbert was suspended for the rest of the 1926 season for failing to exercise the caution which is expected of all seamen. [He did receive a first mate's license for the 1926 season.] The *Dalwarnic*'s first mate was exonerated."

Over the years, we have found a lot of wooden ships, powered by both sail and steam. Our discovery of the *Nisbet Grammer*, one of only two large steel commercial freighters that sank in Lake Ontario, allowed us to scratch that goal off of our list. This was particularly satisfying for Dan who had always wanted to find a major steel hulled vessel.

The *Nisbet Grammer* search team (L-R) Jim Kennard, Roland Stevens, Craig Hampton, and Dan Scoville.
Image courtesy of Jim Kennard

SOURCES:

"Ship of the Month No. 68 *Nisbet Grammer*". *The Scanner*, October 1977. Vol. 10 No. 1.

Canal Boats from 1800s Discovered in Lake Ontario

Our shipwreck exploration team has been surveying large areas of the eastern basin of Lake Ontario since 2011. During that time, we found both commercial sailing vessels and steamers, but that is not all we found! To our surprise, more modern houseboats and 19th century canal boats also populate the bottom of the lake in the eastern basin. Houseboats are designed for travelling on calm water in small lakes, rivers, or canals. However, several people have decided to risk venturing out on to Lake Ontario with their houseboats. We have seen three of these houseboats on the bottom of the lake, two with known loss of life. At the time of discovery, these houseboats were not designated historic as they were not 50 years old. Another surprise discovery in this area of the lake was the presence of canal boats on the lake bottom. Canal boats were designed for use on canals, such as the Erie Canal, where they were towed along the canal by draft animals. They were not designed for open lake travel. We found one canal boat in 2011 and a canal scow[1] a few years later, but we did not formally identify them until 2014, when we were able to put an ROV and technical divers on the wrecks. In that investigation, Roger operated the ROV and technical divers Bob Sherwood and Andrew Driver provided more video and close up inspection of the construction details of the canal boat wrecks.

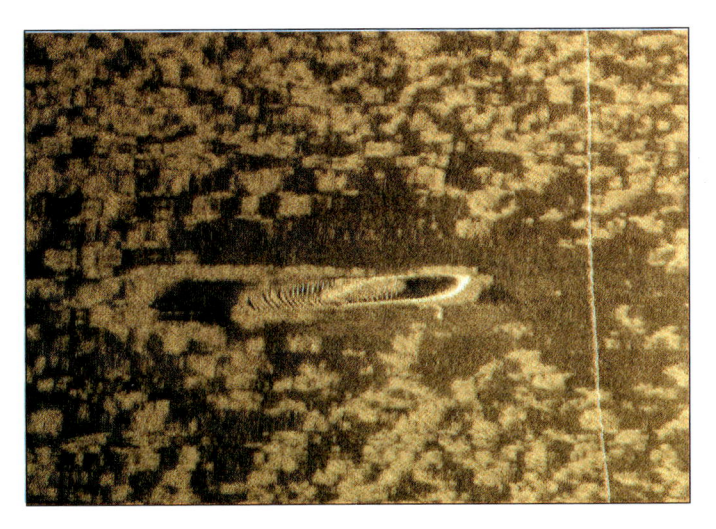

Canal boat side-scan sonar image. Image courtesy of Jim Kennard

---

[1] In the 19th century, scows were often used in the construction of canals and later on issues related to maintenance.

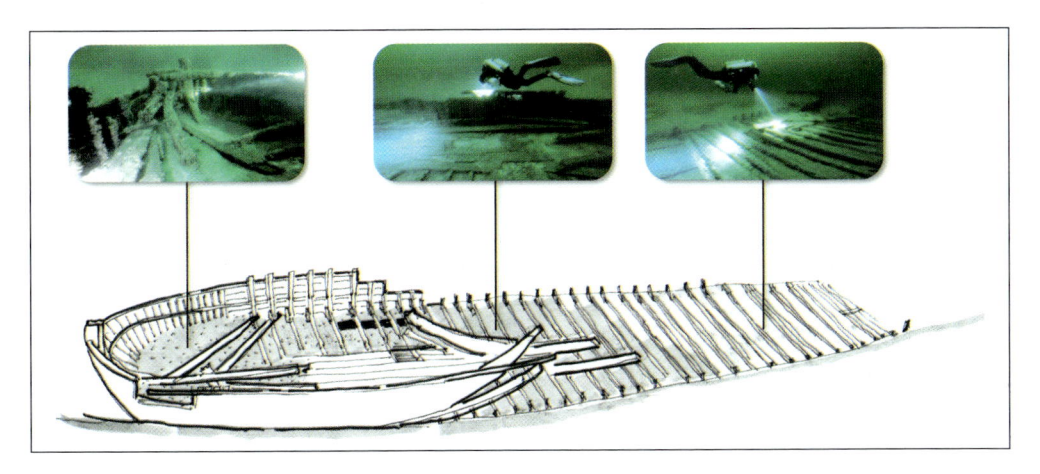

Canal Boats From 1800s Discovered in Lake Ontario

The canal boat wreck. Underwater photos (L-R): looking forward at towing bit, side of vessel with diver, frames.   Drawing by Roland E. Stevens III. Images courtesy of Bob Sherwood

The remains of the small shallow-draft canal boat, 65 feet long with a beam of 14 feet, was discovered in 2011, with a portion of its stern torn away. A review of our side-scan sonar records showed trawl marks on the bottom of the lake that lead right to the stern area of this vessel. Unfortunately, it seems likely that sometime in the past a trawl tore apart the aft portion of this canal boat. There is no evidence of an upper deck, cabin, or any remaining cargo. The vertical frames were attached to the bottom frames with cross braces. Builders of canal boats used a variety of construction designs based on the intended work of the boat. Canal boat builders would not have designed a shallow draft vessel of similar construction to withstand the pounding and stress needed to survive on Lake Ontario during a storm. This canal craft would be fine for travel on the Oswego and Erie Canals but not strong enough for open lake travel on Ontario.

The canal scow has a length of 78 feet and beam of 14 feet and was found with its entire port side torn away. This was a shallow draft vessel of around four feet. Here again, caught in rough conditions while crossing the lake, the shifting cargo probably caused the side of the scow to collapse and the vessel to founder. Both canal boats were found within a few miles of each other on a route approximately midway between Oswego and Sackets Harbor. The depth of both wrecks exceeds 200 feet.

We were not surprised by the fact that neither canal boat had a name board attached to the vessel to aid in identification. I reviewed my database of 600 shipwrecks on Lake Ontario but failed to identify a potential match for either vessel. There are, however, some clues to the time period when

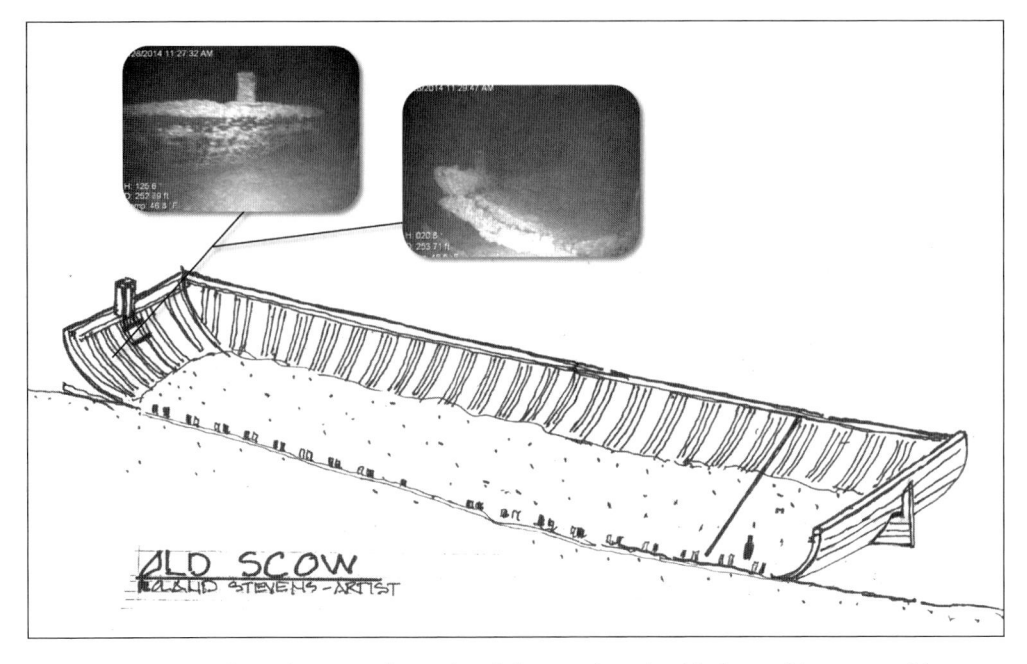

The canal scow wreck. Underwater photos (L-R): bow and towing bit, bow with no port side.
Drawing by Roland E. Stevens III. Images courtesy of Roger Pawlowski

these craft were in operation. The size of both vessels could put their construction in the period from 1850 to 1862, when the Erie Canal system was widened to accommodate boats up to 90 feet in length and 15 feet wide.

I believe that the owners of the canal boat and canal scow decided to tow these vessels by tugboat to transport cargo to or from Oswego or Sackets Harbor. They probably believed that if Lake Ontario was calm, they could make their intended destination without any problems. Unfortunately, the conditions on Lake Ontario change very quickly from calm to high wind and waves. No shallow draft canal boat could survive in those conditions.

There is no record of the loss of these vessels. We believe they were constructed sometime between 1850 and 1875, based on their size relative to the size capacity of the Erie Canal.

EARLY PROPELLER STEAMSHIP *BAY STATE*

Young America, sister ship to the Bay State. Image courtesy of the C. Patrick Labadie Collection / Thunder Bay National Marine Sanctuary, Alpena, Michigan

In late August 2015, we were searching for shipwrecks east of Oswego, when the sonar return of the lake bottom spiked alerting us to a potential shipwreck. We had run over the top of a target, resting deep below on the bottom of the lake. Using our *DeepVision* side-scan sonar, we surveyed the wreck from several different directions to estimate its size and shape to aid in identification. We also surveyed the area around the wreck site and determined that for almost a quarter of a mile the ship came apart leaving debris in its wake before eventually sinking to the bottom of the lake.

Because of the depth of the target, we knew the VideoRay Pro IV remote operated vehicle — capable of descending to a depth of 1,000 feet, with its low-light video camera and onboard lights — was needed. Control and power is provided via a tether attached to the ROV from its control system onboard the boat. We deployed the ROV and landed within 10 yards of the wreck. The onboard sector-scanning sonar guided the ROV to the starboard side of the shipwreck about mid ship. Large pieces of railing or framing hang haphazardly over the wreck. We guided the ROV past these pieces and found a clear area on the deck where it could land and complete a scan of the shipwreck to determine shape and size. In the distance a winch could be seen. The wreck measures 137 feet in length and 27 feet wide.

All of the upper decks of the ship are missing. Only the remains of a rail, or what may have been framing, are left standing mainly in the bow and stern, while other portions are lying on the deck. Two anchors still hang on the starboard and port sides of the bow. As we moved the ROV from the bow to the stern of the ship, something stopped the progress. Extending out from the wreck, a piece of debris snagged the

Side-scan sonar image of *Bay State*.
Image courtesy of Jim Kennard

Bay State underwater. Underwater photos (L-R): starboard anchor, winch, frame debris at midship. Watercolor by Roland E. Stevens III. Images courtesy of Roger Pawlowski

tether of the ROV on a long sliver of wood. The next several hours were spent trying to release the ROV from its entanglement until — eventually — the power from the battery for the ROV ran out. Due to inclement weather in September and lack of availability of technical divers to make a deep dive, nearly a month went by before the ROV was recovered.

Identification of the shipwreck as the *Bay State* was based on several factors including size, shape, type, location, and conditions causing the wreck. When technical divers retrieved the ROV, they had a few minutes to tour the entire shipwreck. They reported viewing the propeller and a large opening on the port side of the ship that would have been used for loading cargo. The *Bay State*'s sister ship, the *Young America*, had similar hatches, which we discovered in an historic photograph of the sister ship. The only propeller-driven steamship designed as a package freighter with side hatches, lost in the area off Fair Haven, New York, of the exact same size as the wreck we discovered is the *Bay State*. The debris trail west of the wreck site provided a clue that the steamship had turned around due to high winds from the west and attempted to make it back to Oswego. Newspaper reports the day after the accident provided information regarding the departure and destination of the *Bay State* and the location of debris found on shore. A review of other steamships lost in Lake Ontario confirms that the *Bay State* is the oldest propeller-driven steamship discovered in the lake through 2018.

The first Great Lakes propeller-driven steamship to carry passengers and freight was built in 1841, at Oswego, New York. In November of that year, that steamship — the *Vandalia* — made its first trial run on Lake Ontario. The *Vandalia* was a "steam sloop" with passenger cabins built on the main deck. In 1842, the *Vandalia* passed through the Welland Canal and began its commercial business on the Great Lakes. Prior to 1841, steamships on the Lakes were driven by paddlewheels, which limited their ability to pass through the Welland Canal due to their added width from the side paddlewheels. With the arrival of the *Vandalia*, it was possible for goods carried by propeller steamships to be shipped directly to ports in Lake Ontario from Lake Erie and the Upper Lakes without offloading at Buffalo. Over the next several years, more propeller steamships were built at Oswego, Buffalo, Cleveland, and Perrysburg, many of which would support the transportation of goods shipped up the Oswego River from the Erie Canal for delivery to the Lake Erie and beyond. The *Bay State* was one of those ships.

The steamship *Bay State* was built in Buffalo, New York, in 1852, by shipbuilders Bidwell & Banta. The Northern Transportation Company owned the ship in 1861.[1] As indicated on the enrollment papers, the steamship was a wooden ship, 137 feet long, with a beam of 26 feet, two decks, and a single mast. The *Bay State* was one of the earliest propeller-driven steamships on the Great Lakes. Based on a variety of on-line sources, between 11 and 30 such vessels were constructed prior to 1852.

It was nearly midnight on Monday, November 2, 1862, when the steamship *Bay State,* captained by William Marshall, departed Oswego, New York, with a full cargo of general merchandise for Cleveland and Toledo. Soon after, winds from the west increased to gale force preventing the steamer from making headway to the Welland Canal. Onboard the *Bay State* were 10 passengers, plus officers and crew. There were no records kept of the crew so the exact number of those lost is not known. Based on the pieces of wreckage found on the floor of the lake, it appears that Captain William Marshall turned the *Bay State* around and headed back to Oswego. Tragically the *Bay State* started to come apart, depositing pieces of the ship on the bottom of the lake. Within a quarter mile the steamship foundered. Wreckage and merchandise washed ashore at Oswego. Cartloads of goods were gathered up by eager residents and quickly carried away. The lifeboat and many papers from the steamer came ashore about three miles west of the city. Unfortunately, none of the passengers or crew survived this terrible marine disaster.

Lost on the Steamer *Bay State*

Officers and Crew:
William Marshall, Jr., Captain — Clayton, New York
Ebenezer Elliot, First Mate — Cleveland, Ohio.
Nathaniel Tacklebury, Second Mate — Ogdensburg, New York
Cornelius Matthewson, First Engineer — Detroit, Michigan
Francis P. Fisher, Second Engineer — Detroit, Michigan
William Murray, Wheelsman — Ogdensburg. New York
John Levis, Wheelsman — Prescott, Ontario
Henry Pero, Fireman — Ogdensburg, New York
James Coss, Fireman — Prescott, Ontario
Emile Marceau, Watchman — Ogdensburg, New York

---

[1] Ownership information is found primarily in annual vessel enrollment papers but sometimes, when these enrollments are transcribed for digital reproduction, errors are made. The *Bay State*, according to one research website, was owned by Chamberlain and Crawford in 1861. However, this might be a transcription error, as other research sources list different owners in 1861.

Donti Marceau, Porter — Ogdensburg, New York (son of Watchman)
C. A. McLeace, Steward — Cleveland, Ohio
Mary McLeace, Stewardess — Cleveland, Ohio
John Wilson, Deckhand — Prescott, Ontario
Patrick Coady, Deckhand — Buffalo, New York
Mr. Galiber, Deckhand — Prescott, New York

Cabin Passengers:
Orley Thomson, Richmond, Vermont (Nephew of John T, Crawford, agent of the Northern Transportation Co.)
Mrs. Scruton and child going to meet her husband at Port Colborne, Ontario
Four women from Brockville, Ontario, going to Ohio to meet their husbands or friends with three little boys

We ended a successful 2015 search season by reaching our goal of finding at least one new shipwreck, although we almost lost a very expensive ROV. Aside from the cost of hiring technical divers to make its recovery, we also lost the use of a $2,500 ROV grabber arm, which flooded and was damaged beyond repair while on the bottom for six weeks. We could only hope that the 2016 shipwreck search season would be more productive and much less costly than this year.

SOURCES:

Oswego Commercial Times, November 4, 1862.
New York Reformer [Jefferson County, New York], November 20, 1862.

Canadian Schooner *Royal Albert* "Derailed" in Lake Ontario

In 2016, our efforts in the first few months of the search season were disappointing. By late June, as in the past, our patience paid off. Using the *DeepVision* side-scan sonar, we were blessed with an image leaving no question that we had discovered a large two-masted schooner off Fair Haven, New York. We spent the next several hours surveying the shipwreck from several different directions with the side-scan sonar to determine its size and shape. We also surveyed the area around the wreck site to determine if pieces of the ship had fallen off and were resting nearby on the lake floor. The side-scan sonar not only helps to identify the wreck, but can provide critical information needed to safely put the ROV on the site. As we saw earlier, an ROV snagged on a shipwreck pretty much spells the end of the search season!

Side-scan sonar image of the *Royal Albert*.
Image courtesy of Jim Kennard

Typically, there is very little light in the deep waters where we find shipwrecks. In the past, we tried using the lights on the ROV, but often experienced back scatter distortion of the video images. For better imaging, we now placed a 25,000 lumen underwater light approximately 30 feet over the middle of the shipwreck.[1] Once the underwater light is in place, we deploy the ROV. Over the years, we used different ROVs, each with different capabilities, as the technology evolved. The VideoRay Pro IV has two video cameras on board, one with standard video, used to monitor topside on the boat; the other, a high-definition camera that records video on a memory chip.

We positioned the drop light perfectly above the center of the shipwreck, which provided very good illumination all the way from the bow and stern of the ship. During the side-scan sonar survey, we determined

---

[1] This method of lighting up the boat from above requires a drop line to which we attach the independent lighting.

that the wreck was around 100 feet long. The ROV survey gave us great details about the wreck's current condition. Both masts are present but not standing. The forward mast is lying off the starboard side of the ship and the mainmast is back off the port side. The boom of the mainmast lies across the cabin roof. The schooner's anchors are still in place on either side of the bow. Toward the bow there is a large winch in front of the displaced forward mast. Behind it, a large hatch is open, but completely filled with sediment. At mid ship, a small hatch is present. Between the mainmast's original location and the cabin is a long aft hatch. Long iron rails are partially hanging out of the aft hold. In the stern area, there is a large amount of wreckage. It is possible that the rails in the aft hold shifted toward the stern end of the schooner, tearing open the ship and allowing water to rush in, ultimately sinking her.

After reviewing our database of over 600 shipwrecks in Lake Ontario, we found only one schooner with two masts that sank off the Fair Haven area with the dimensions we had measured and carrying a cargo of railroad rails, this was the schooner *Royal Albert*.

The schooner *Royal Albert* was built in 1858, in Oakville, Ontario, by shipbuilder, John Simpson. In 1849, John and his brother, Melancthon,

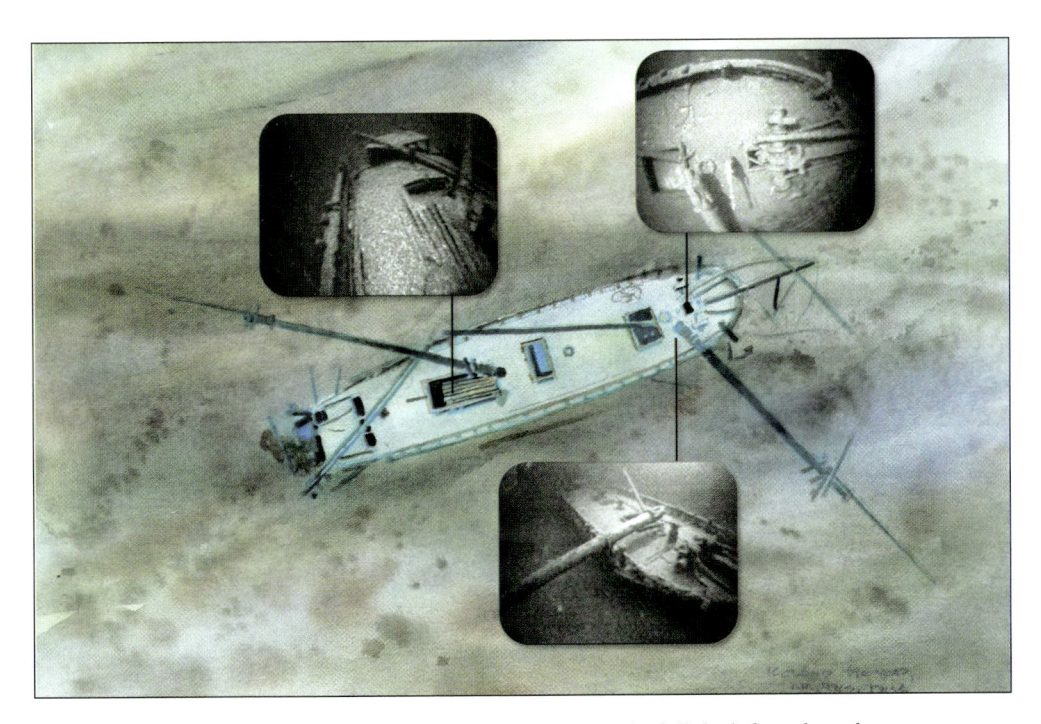

Royal Albert. Underwater photos (L-R): aft hold showing rails, full deck from bow, bow. Watercolor by Roland E. Stevens III. Images courtesy of Roger Pawlowski

established a shipbuilding operation in that small port with its good harbor protected by two manmade piers that were built in 1830. The first ship the brothers built was the schooner *Catherine*. The Simpsons continued to build sailing ships in Oakville and in the neighboring ports of Bronte and Burlington until 1863 when they moved closer to the Welland Canal.

> The Canadian registration of the schooner *Royal Albert* provides the original builder information as follows:
>
> Length: 103.66 ft.
> Beam: 23 ft.
> Depth: 8.83 ft.
> Tons: 165
> Stern: Square
> Masts: Two
> Built: Oakville, Ontario, Canada
> Date: 1858

The *Royal Albert* had several Canadian owners in the 10 years that she sailed:

1858 — John Simpson and Company, Oakville, Ontario.
September 26, 1861 — Thomas C. Chisholm, Benjamin Hagaman & Noah Brinhest, Toronto, Ontario; 165 tons
October 10, 1865 — John Dench, Trenton, Ontario; 174 gross tons
October 24, 1866 — Robert G. Post, Pickering, Ontario
1868 — H. C. Bolland, Oswego, New York; 159 gross tons

On Friday evening, August 7, 1868, the *Royal Albert*, commanded by Captain Peter Conley, departed Oswego, New York, loaded with 285 tons of railroad rails. She was headed due west for the Welland Canal and then on to Toledo, Ohio, to deliver her cargo. Underway for just a few hours, she was off Fair Haven when she sank rapidly. The crew barely had enough time to launch a yawl for their escape. Fortunately, they were successful in making it to shore the next morning arriving at Oswego in the small boat. The *Royal Albert* was considered a well-constructed and safe vessel. The rapidity of her loss led to speculation on the part of the crew as to what may have caused the disaster. Our survey confirms the crew's speculation that the railroad rails had either shifted toward the aft end of the ship puncturing a hole in the stern, or had caused seams in the hull to burst, thus allowing water to rapidly fill the holds causing the schooner *Royal Albert* to founder.

The last owner, H. C. Bolland of Oswego, New York, appears to have acquired the ship less than a year before it was lost. It was known at the time that Bolland had just made the schooner ready for the fall season. The *Royal Albert* was sold to Mr. Bolland for $10,000 but was insured for only $7,000.

The feelings generated by the discovery and identification of a shipwreck vary for so many different reasons. In the case of the *Royal Albert*, being able to see the culprit that caused the loss of the vessel, in this case the shifting rails, was particularly satisfying. It also helped to inspire a good chapter title!

SOURCES:

Buffalo Commercial Advertiser, August 10, 1868.
Canadian Ship Registrations. Library and Archives Canada.
Chicago Tribune, August 12, 1868.
Oswego Advertiser & Times, August 8, 1868.
St. Lawrence Republican [Ogdensburg, New York], August 11, 1868.

DISCOVERY OF A GREAT LAKES TREASURE: SLOOP *WASHINGTON*

Sloop *Washington* under sail.   Watercolor by Roland E. Stevens III

When I began searching for shipwrecks, I have to admit I was motivated by a monetary interest. I wanted to find a shipwreck that had not been discovered, salvaged, or disrupted and better yet, that had some type of treasure on board. In my youth, tales of the discovery of treasure from Spanish Galleons on the Atlantic fueled this desire. Unfortunately, claims of treasure ships on the Great Lakes made by many an author turned out to be unsubstantiated. Perhaps those authors were driven by financial interest as well! Even the HMS *Ontario*, with rumors of a $500,00 payroll onboard, turned out to be myth when subjected to serious research.

In June 2016, the current team consisting of Roger, Roland, and myself were searching under The Explorers Club Expedition Flag #202 for shipwrecks in deep water off Oswego, New York.[1] We had just started our search

---

[1] In 2013, I was nominated and elected as a Fellow in The Explorers' Club. In 2016, the Club endorsed our search with an expedition flag.

grid, when we came upon what appeared to be a sunken sloop, a small single-masted vessel. We made a number of passes with the side-scan but the conditions were not ideal for deploying an ROV. Our previous research suggested that the sloop *Washington* sank in these deep waters in 1803. From the sonar imagery, we thought we had found the *Washington,* but had to wait another three weeks before lake conditions were good enough for imaging with the ROV, which could help confirm our identification.

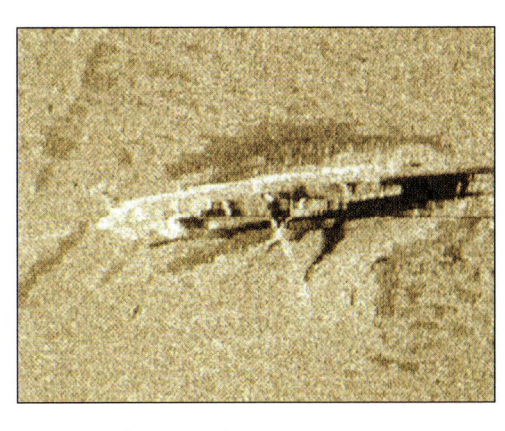

Sloop *Washington* side-scan sonar image.
Image courtesy of Jim Kennard

To obtain the best images of the shipwreck, we needed to wait for a very calm day when the sun would be directly overhead. This method allows natural light to illuminate a wreck so the entire ship can be captured in the video image. We deployed the ROV and started at the bow of the shipwreck where — suddenly — a long protruding bowsprit points directly at us on the screen. Roger piloted the ROV following the bowsprit aft to the starboard side of the ship where an anchor hangs on the side of the hull. Moving up to the deck, the chain plates are clearly visible. In the bow area is a wooden windlass, now covered with quagga mussels, as is almost all of the ship. A small hold is located just forward of the windlass. The single mast of the sloop is still standing tall, but the sails and rigging have long since rotted away. Just behind the mast is another hold, larger than the one in the bow area. Behind that hold are the remains of a double bilge pump. The cabin is extensively damaged with its roof lying just off to the port side of the ship. The long boom for the mainsail lies across the deck and off to the port side. As the ROV approached the aft end of the ship, it became obvious that the sloop must have gone down stern first, as there is considerable damage in that area. We hypothesized that the cabin roof was probably

Starboard side of *Washington.*
Image courtesy of Roger Pawlowski

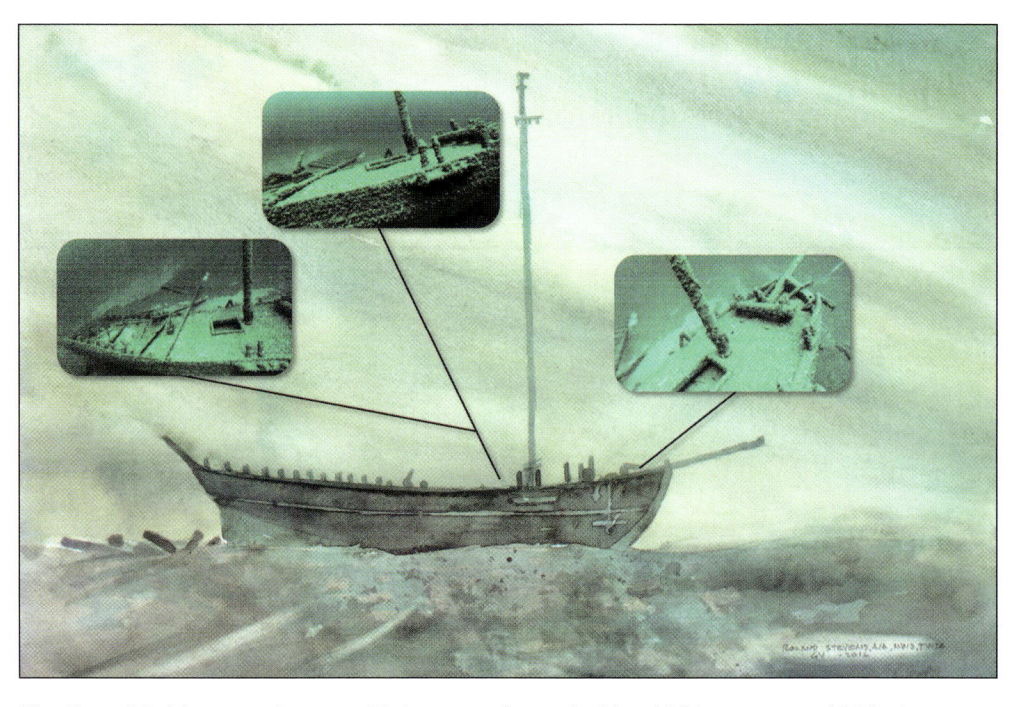

Shipwrecks of Lake Ontario: A Journey of Discovery

The Sloop *Washington* underwater. Underwater photos (L-R): midship to stern, midship, bow.
Watercolor by Roland E. Stevens III. Images courtesy of Roger Pawlowski

Windlass on the *Washington*.
Image courtesy of Roger Pawlowski

Mast top of the *Washington*.
Image courtesy of Roger Pawlowski

torn off when the sloop hit the lake floor. After the initial wreck survey, Roger maneuvered the ROV to the middle of the ship and set it down on the deck. He then took a radar-like image of the sloop with the sector-scanning sonar mounted on the ROV from which we were able to obtain precise measurements. The overall length of the sloop is 53 feet with a beam of 16½ feet. We estimate that the depth of the sloop from the deck to the bottom of the keel is approximately 9 feet. With these measurements, we were able to confirm the identity of the ship as the sloop *Washington*.

Construction of the sloop *Washington* began in 1797, on Fourmile Creek, near present day Erie, Pennsylvania, by Connecticut carpenter Eliphalet Beebe for the Pennsylvania Population Company, an organization that was developing a tract of land just north of current day Erie. The *Washington* was a small sloop with a carrying capacity of 36 tons. The sloop was initially built to transport people, their belongings and supplies from both New York and Canada to the tract of land owned by the Pennsylvania Population Company. On September 15, 1798, the sloop was launched at Fourmile Creek. Its maiden voyage was to Fort Erie for supplies. The Pennsylvania Population Company took ownership of the sloop a month later on October 12. Two names were proposed for the sloop, *Washington* and *Lady Washington*. The name *Washington* was chosen by the ship's largest shareholder, Robert Hamilton, a merchant from Queenston, Ontario. It appears, however, that the sloop continued to be referred to as *Lady Washington* by some causing confusion to some treasure book writers as to the correct name of the sloop — *Washington*.

Sloop *Washington* during portage to Lake Ontario.   Drawing by Mark Peckham

For the next three years, the *Washington* sailed the eastern end of Lake Erie making frequent trips to Fort Erie to move merchandise and settlers between New York State, Canada, and Erie, Pennsylvania. By the end of the 1800 season, the sloop was losing money and was put up for sale. In November 1801, the *Washington* was sold to a group of merchants from Queenston, Ontario. In the winter of 1802, the sloop was transported around Niagara Falls, over the portage road (a trail on land between two bodies of water) from Chippawa to Queenston and launched in Lake Ontario. This feat makes the sloop *Washington* the first ship ever to have sailed in both Lakes Erie and Ontario. For the portage, the ship was mounted on runners and, with the use of rollers, pulled by teams of oxen for a distance of approximately eight miles to its destination. Today, the trail between Chippawa and Queenston, called Portage Road, carries cars and trucks.

For the next two years, the *Washington* transported furs and local merchants from Queenston to Kingston, Ontario. The sloop would return to its homeport with an assortment of goods such as flour, salt, tools, and household items. Records from 1803 suggest that the *Washington* was making a trip nearly every month to Kingston starting in early April until its final voyage in early November.

On November 6, 1803, the *Washington* sailed out of Kingston Harbor on her final return trip to Niagara. Onboard was the crew of Captain Murray, Peter Bouville, and John Neach, along with several passengers including Niagara merchants John Dun and John Boyd. After their departure, a severe storm developed on Lake Ontario. Other sailing vessels arrived at Niagara

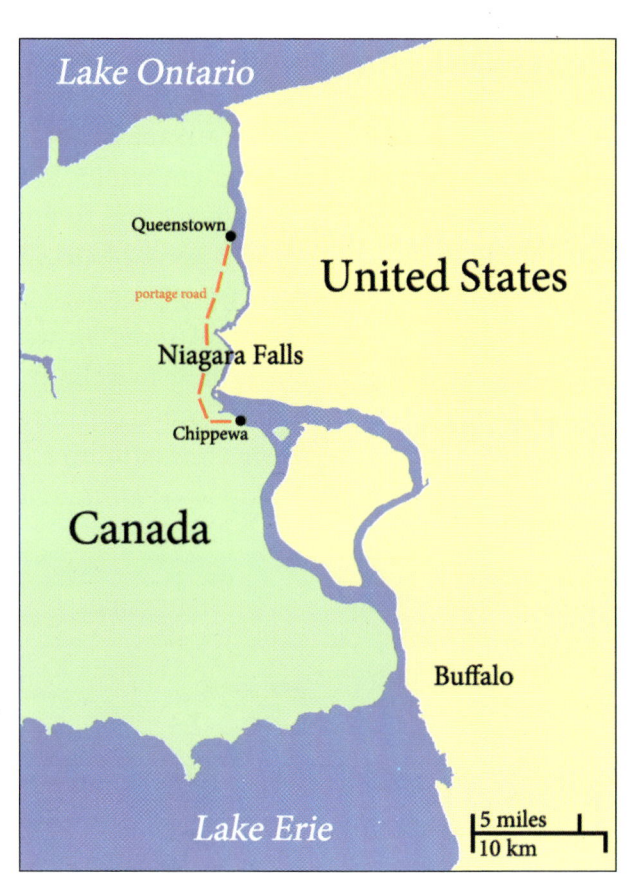

Map of the Niagara River showing the portage route of the sloop *Washington*

and not finding the *Washington* assumed that she had made it to the port of Oswego, New York. Soon afterwards, ships coming from that port brought the news that several articles of cargo, pieces of wreckage, and the *Washington*'s yawl were found on shore near Oswego.

An advertisement published in the *Upper Canada Gazette* on December 10, 1803, by Mr. Quetton St. George (merchant from York [Toronto, Canada] who owned a large portion of the cargo aboard the sloop *Washington*), provides our best description of the type of material being transported. It reads: "Mr. St. George is very sorry that he has not received his East India goods and groceries. He is sure they are at Oswego and should they not arrive this season they may be looked for early in the spring." The cargo, with an estimated value of $20,000, had been purchased by Messrs. Robinson and Martin of Albany, New York, and Mr. St. George.

As of 2018, the sloop *Washington* is the oldest commercial sailing vessel to have been lost and found in the Great Lakes. The fact that she was the first vessel to sail in both Lake Erie and Lake Ontario only adds to the importance of the discovery. Since no plans or half hull from her construction exist, the measurements and imagery of our survey provide archaeologists and students of naval architecture with the opportunity to more fully understand the design of a rare, late 18th century sailing vessel. I have since come to realize that the real treasure aboard these shipwrecks is the *historic treasure* and that any monetary treasure is only found on the pages of the shipwreck treasure books.

SOURCES:

Albany Gazette, December 19, 1803.
Merritt, Richard, Nancy Butler, and Michael Power, eds. *The Capital Years: Niagara-on-the-Lake, 1792-1796.* Toronto: Dundurn Press, 1991.
Pennsylvania Population Company document collection. Erie County Historical Society.
Upper Canada Gazette [Ontario], November 16, 1803.
_____, December 10, 1803.

REMAINS OF THE SCHOONER *HARTFORD* FOUND

Several times each season, our exploration team makes a trip to Mexico Bay in search of shipwrecks. Nearly all the ships that wrecked in Mexico Bay did so very near shore in the shallows. The depths in the Mexico Bay area are such that recreational diving (less than 135 feet) is possible. Almost all of the wrecks we have discovered over the past several decades have been in deep water, beyond the limits of recreational diving. We felt Mexico Bay provided the best opportunity to find wrecks that could be explored by members of the recreational diving community. That is not to say this was our only motivation. We knew that a C-47 aircraft had crashed in June 1944, off Sandy Pond not far from shore. Now that would be something of interest. In addition, a fisherman reported an oil slick on the water off Ramona Beach while retrieving his nets, leading some to believe that a B-24 that crashed in the lake with eight crewmen on board in February 1944, could be in this area.

In 2013, while conducting a sonar search off the area of Sandy Pond, we found a very interesting circular-shaped object in 30 feet of water. Wow!! Could this be part of the C-47 aircraft? That day, a swift breeze was blowing, which made it a bit difficult for the anchor to hold on the sandy bottom, but after several attempts, the boat finally held fast. Although the target was only 30 feet below, we deployed the ROV as we did not have any dive gear with us. With great anticipation, the ROV moved in on the target only to discover that we had found a large round rock. Disappointing! We resumed our search and within a few hours another target appeared at a depth of 40 feet. This time there was no mistaking the side-scan sonar image — it was part of a shipwreck. We once again deployed the ROV and began to

Side-sonar image of the *Hartford*.
Image courtesy of Jim Kennard

video the remains of the hull of a wooden ship. Unfortunately, the visibility was limited to about four or five feet due to the previous day's high winds stirring up the lake bottom. From what we could discern, it appeared that we were looking at the middle portion of the hull of a ship that did not protrude more than a foot off the lake bottom. The sides had fallen away and pieces of them lay nearby. The stern and the bow were not in evidence. The remains of the hull were essentially flattened with only a few ribs remaining. This area off Sandy Pond has a huge amount of shifting sand and heavy ice floes during the winter. It was quite surprising to me considering the shallow depth, wave action, and ice movement that anything could still remain from this shipwreck.

As the reader has seen throughout this book, shipwreck identification is often complicated. For this target, with the help of Mark Barbour, a longtime diver and researcher, we determined that this discovery was part of the hull of the *Hartford*, a three-masted schooner that foundered in Mexico Bay. The *Hartford* disaster was widely reported in local newspapers, which included statements from witnesses on shore and the experiences of members of the local lifesaving station. With such data in hand, making her identification was relatively simple.

On October 5, 1894, the schooner *Hartford* sailed from Detroit, Michigan, destined for Cape Vincent in the St. Lawrence River with 22,000 bushels of wheat consigned to Farwell & Rhins of Watertown, New York. Four days later, the ship passed through the Welland Canal and anchored off Toronto Point until noon the next day while waiting for the headwinds from the east to abate. By Thursday morning October 11, the *Hartford* was off Oswego. The captain of the schooner *Mystic Star* observed the *Hartford* as she sailed by the Oswego Harbor. He was of the opinion that her steering gear was either damaged or not working at all. He remarked, "she was making a zig-zag course, first heading to shore then steering off into the lake…" However, she offered no distress signal. Another person who was observing the *Hartford* through a powerful marine glass saw the schooner about 8 or 10 miles out in the lake steering very badly. At one o'clock in the afternoon, the *Hartford* was in Mexico Bay. By now the winds had picked up again and were blowing at gale force out of the northwest upwards of 50 miles per hour. One of the first to see the schooner was a Mrs. Eugene Bartlett who watched the tragedy unfold through a powerful telescope. The vessel came closer to shore, as though it was trying to make it to the mouth of Little Sandy Creek, then turned back out into the lake trying to work its way out of Mexico Bay.

Soon afterwards, the ship disappeared in a heavy squall of rain and mist for about 20 minutes. When it lifted, her sailors were busy on deck when suddenly a huge wave hit the schooner broadside rolling the ship over on her side. Three times the schooner righted itself. Then, a wave much larger than the others struck the *Hartford* on the port side and she went over on

Unidentified shipwrecks, men clinging to a mast during a storm.
Watercolor by Roland E. Stevens III

her beam ends causing the mainmast and topmast to come out of the deck. The spars were carried away and the crew disappeared. At this point, the *Hartford* was estimated to be one and a half to two miles from shore.

An hour earlier, one of the crew from the Big Sandy Lifesaving station had also been watching the schooner and he judged her to be three to four miles from shore. He observed, "she was going along under a flying jib, jib staysail, a whole foresail, a single reefed mainsail, and a double reefed mizzen." He watched her for half an hour but she was not making any headway. He watched as the *Hartford*'s crew took in the jib and lowered the other sails to the deck. The crew let the anchors go but it appeared that they were dragging along on the bottom. At this point, he reported the situation to the lifesaving station captain who ordered the men to go up the shore with the beach apparatus. In a short time, they watched the schooner roll over on its side. The captain then redirected the men to return to the station and get the lifeboat. It was a tremendous effort on the part of the lifesaving crew to pull their vessel five miles through the breakers in the face of the wind and waves. Three hours later, the lifesaving men arrived at the beach opposite the wreck but they did not see any of the *Hartford*'s crew. Around 4 p.m., the mast gave way and the wreck was no longer visible. Then some of the wreckage began to come ashore. When the lifesaving station men started back to the station, three hatches, a yawl, a tub, spars, stools, and brooms had made their way to the shore.

During the night, the Pulaski sheriff and several individuals patrolled the beach area. At 11 p.m., the body of Captain O'Toole's five-month-old child was found on the shore among the wreckage. During the night, locals carried off most of the items coming to shore, including the cabin furniture, chairs, bedding, hatches, a stern post, yawl, and bow sprit. By morning it appeared as if a swarm of locusts had cleaned the beach of most of the debris leaving only the broken yawl, masts, rudder, and the ship's cabin. The sails were seen floating on the water still connected to the shipwreck.

The next day, the lifesaving crew was able to reach the vicinity of the shipwreck and determined that there was nothing left to be saved. Nine days later, the body of Mary O'Toole, the captain's wife, was found floating about two miles south of the wreck site and three miles from shore. Five children of Captain O'Toole and his wife Mary, ages 2 to 11, were now orphans.

Captain William and Mary O'Toole

LOST ON THE SCHOONER *HARTFORD*:

William O'Toole, Captain — Clayton, New York
Mary O'Toole, Wife — Clayton, New York
Mary Kathleen O'Toole, Daughter — Clayton New York
Damus Turgeon, Mate — Clayton, New York
William Donaldson, Mate — Thurso, New York
Mr. Farauhaurson — Grindstone Island, New york
Dennis McCarthy — Oswego, New York

NOTE: Initial reports by the local newspapers indicated that Michael Purcell of Clayton, New York and Richard Seymour, both sailors, had perished on the *Hartford*. Several days later, it was found that they had taken their leave on an earlier voyage and were safe.

In mid-November, part of the *Hartford*'s hull had been driven ashore in Mexico Bay. As the month came to a close, the steamer *Coaster* from Cape Vincent arrived at the *Hartford* wreck site with a diver to inspect the sunken vessel. The wreck of the *Hartford* was lying on her keel in 40 feet of water. Sails and lines covered a portion of the deck. The decks were broken and bulging outward from the force of the swelling grain. One anchor lay on the deck and the other nearby on the lake bottom. There was no way to get into the cargo hold due to the amount of the grain that had swelled up. There were no bodies found on the wreck. The diver spent nearly 45 minutes inspecting the wreck. After an assessment of the ship's condition, the principal owner, C. W. McKinley, indicated that he would wait until the spring to raise her.

In 1971, divers found the remains of the portion of the hull of the *Hartford* that I rediscovered in 2013. In 1972, there was an effort underway by the Thousand Island Shipyard Museum (now Antique Boat Museum) to raise the remains of the hull and have it restored with the help of the Syracuse SCUBA club. The director of the museum, Thomas Turgeon, was the grandson of Damus Turgeon, one of the *Hartford*'s crew. New York State issued the appropriate permit but no funds were available for the salvage work. Ultimately, the Corps of Army Engineers did not approve the plan and the project was abandoned. At this writing, that piece of hull still remains and is a home for small lake fish.

SOURCES:

Oswego Daily Palladium, October 12, 1894.
_____, October 13, 1894.
_____, October 15, 1894.
_____, November 1, 1894.
_____, November 17, 1894.
Sandy Creek News, October 18, 1894.
_____, November 1, 1894.
Watertown Daily Times, October 11, 1894.
_____, March 18, 1972.
_____, May 15, 1972.

Schooner *Hartford*.
Image courtesy Historical Collection of the Great Lakes at Bowling Green State University

The *Hartford*, a three-masted canal schooner, was built in Gibraltar, Michigan, by Linn & Craig Company in 1873. In 1884, the schooner was sold to W. H. Consaul, G.H. McKinley of Cape Vincent and Captain William A. O'Toole of Clayton.
Official No. 95229
Length: 137.5'
Width: 26'
Depth: 11'
Tonnage: 307 gross
Hull: Wood

Rare Sailing Craft Found in Lake Ontario

Black Duck Under Sail.   Drawing by Mark Peckham

In May 2013, we returned to the deep waters north of Oswego as our target area for the season. In that month, we ran right over the top of what appeared to be the mast of a shipwreck with our side-scan sonar. In early July of that year, we returned to the target and deployed a small ROV to survey the ship. The ROV reached one side of the ship but the extreme depth compressed the neutrally buoyant cable, causing it act as a weight. This situation restricted movement of the ROV and we could only glimpse the rail and mast — too little to hypothesize about this discovery. In September 2016, with a *VideoRay Pro IV* ROV and an improved cable tether, the team decided to go back to the unknown shipwreck we located three years earlier. This time, the team was able to successfully survey the shipwreck.

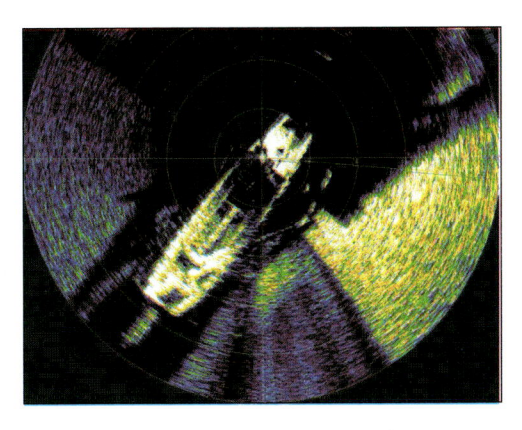

The shipwreck lies in nearly 350 feet of water. To illuminate the ship, we lowered a 25,000 lumen light just above the shipwreck, as we did on the *Royal Albert*. The ship has a single mast which is still standing. Behind the mast is a single large hatch with a centerboard trunk in its middle. This holds a pivoted centerboard that could be extended through the keel to provide greater stability when sailing in the open lake. The bow is squared off, being only a few feet less in width than the squared off stern. A short bow sprit extends from the bow. The anchor hangs from the bow. The cabin rises up from the deck by a few feet and is just about as wide as the ship. A tiller lies across the cabin roof. Portions of the sides of the cabin have fallen away. The davits that held the ship's punt (a small boat propelled with a

Sector-sonar image of the *Black Duck*.
Image courtesy of Roger Pawlowski

Black Duck with the squared off scow bow.
Image courtesy of Roger Pawlowski

Black Duck, cabin and tiller.
Image courtesy of Roger Pawlowski

Stern of the *Black Duck*.   Image courtesy of Roger Pawlowski

pole), extend beyond the end of the stern. Below them, the rudder can be seen mostly buried in the lake bottom.

After reviewing the underwater video, the team concluded that we had found a scow sloop, a rare sailing vessel that began to appear on the Great Lakes around 1825. The scow sloop was a shallow-draft sailing ship having a single mast, flat bottom, and a squared off bow and stern. The combination of the scow-shaped hull and the sail plan of the sloop is what makes this ship unusual, as there were more schooner-rigged scows in the Great Lakes. Scow sloops are a very simple design, cheaply built, and their length ranges from 22 feet to over 95 feet. Typically the scow sloop was utilized on rivers or short lake crossings for the transportation of lumber, sand, hay, and coal to ports that did not have a deep harbor. They could even be easily run up on a beach to offload their cargoes. They were not constructed to withstand the high winds and waves on the open lake. There were a few scow sloops that were used in the Upper Great Lakes but most were found working on the eastern end of Lake Ontario and the St. Lawrence River. The scow sloop appears to have been a common vessel in many places including Lake Champlain, the Connecticut and Hudson Rivers, as well as all along the Atlantic Coast. With our hypothesis of this shipwreck being a scow sloop in hand, the team reviewed shipwreck databases to begin winnowing down the field of possible ships. The scow sloop *Black Duck* quickly rose to the top of the list.

The *Black Duck* was built on Wellesley Island on the St. Lawrence River in 1859, by C. Pearson Harrison. In 1870, Sackets Harbor merchants Barney Everleigh and John Jackson purchased her. She was a small shallow draft vessel with a length of 51 feet, beam of 13 feet, and depth of only 4 feet. The *Black Duck* had a rated carrying capacity of a little over 21 tons.

Black Duck in distress.   Drawing by Mark Peckham

The *Black Duck* was loaded with a cargo of coal and general merchandise when it left Oswego, New York, for Sackets Harbor a little past noon Friday, August 2, 1872. A strong wind was blowing during her departure, but Captain Barney Everleigh believed that he could make the 40 mile trip by midnight. Within a few hours, the winds changed and the little scow sloop was sailing broadside to the northwest gale force winds. The captain changed course to steer up the lake to prevent the waves from coming over the side of the ship just as it sprung a severe leak. The *Black Duck* rapidly began to take on water. The pumps were manned but could not handle the flow of the incoming water. Captain Everleigh, his wife, his brother, and crewmember Willie Decker, prepared to leave the sinking ship. The small punt was cut loose prematurely and began to float away. Decker dove into the water and swam to the punt, securing it before it was blown out of reach. Captain Everleigh and his wife jumped from the sinking ship and swam to the punt arriving near exhaustion. The captain's brother also made it to the small boat. For the next eight hours, three of them lay in the bottom of the punt while the fourth rowed. Eventually, the wind blew them to shore about two miles north of Port Ontario, New York.

Based on the data collected from the side-scan sonar and ROV, we believe our target matches closely the official dimensions of the *Black Duck*. The missing punt fits well with the firsthand accounts of the disaster that we located. Finding a shipwreck that is well known is certainly its own reward. However, the little *Black Duck* was equally satisfying because it may be the only fully-intact scow sloop shipwreck found on the Great Lakes. In the shipwreck discovery business, notoriety is great but our video of the *Black Duck* has added to the naval architect's understanding of the rare Lake Ontario scow sloop typology.

Source:

Jefferson County Journal [Adams, New York], August 8, 1872.

APPENDICES

FORD SHOALS: A MOST DANGEROUS PLACE

It has been remarked that one of the most dangerous places in Lake Ontario is Ford Shoals. Located four-and-one-half miles west of Oswego, the shoal area is a shelf of rock that extends nearly half a mile out into the lake. The water depth in some of the shoal area is only three to four feet, depending on the lake levels. From the 1830s into the early 1900s, a number of sailing ships, steamers, and canal boats were severely damaged or totally wrecked on Ford Shoals, which was originally named Ford's Shoal on an 1836 navigation chart created for the US Navy by Augustus Ford who conducted the early 1800s survey of Lake Ontario. Perhaps Augustus gave the shoal his family name as tribute to his past extensive survey work on that rock shelf. Ford was one of the early Oswego settlers who lived three miles west in Unionville and close to the shoal area. Over time, Augustus explored the shoal and provided the first details of this area on the US Navy chart of Lake Ontario. During a 12-year period, Ford surveyed all of Lake Ontario in both US and British (Canadian) waters. The USN 1836 chart is not nearly as precise as that now produced by NOAA, but it certainly was a good chart to have, especially when navigating near the shore of Lake Ontario.

    In general, the southern shore of Lake Ontario drops off fairly quickly into depths greater than 10 feet which was enough for sailing ships and most steamers of the time. Ships usually got into trouble coming from the west and heading to the Oswego Harbor. If they did not stay more than half a mile from shore, they would most likely end up in danger of being

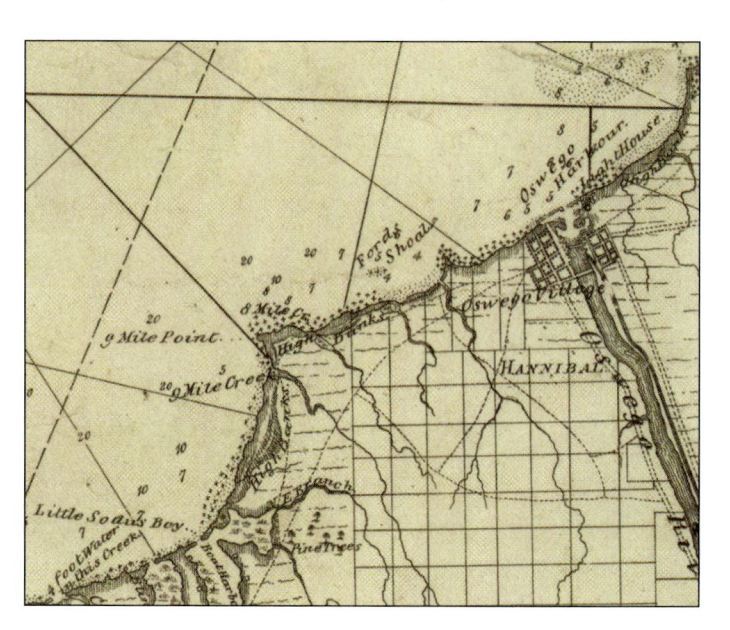

1836 map showing Ford Shoals.   *Image courtesy of Jim Kennard*

grounded on Ford Shoals. After over 50 years of ships becoming stranded or wrecked on the shoals, a US vessel owners' association proposed legislation that called for a buoy to be placed on Ford Shoals. The request was approved and by 1903, a large 25-foot black spar buoy was anchored on the outer north end of the shoal in 17 feet of water. This did not totally stop ships from being stranded or wrecked on Ford Shoals, as a few more met their end in the next 20 years. In 1930, the spar buoy was changed to a special can buoy with reflectors on top; in 1932, this was changed to a buoy with a bell. It appears that many of the groundings on Ford Shoals were due to poor visibility in snowstorms, especially when operating at the very end of the shipping season, or in a few situations due to a very heavy fog. Today not much can be found on Ford Shoals except the ground-down remains of the steamer *David W. Mills*, which is described in a later chapter, "Recreational Diving on Shipwrecks Near Oswego.") Wave action and ice removed much of the remnants of ships whose hulls had not previously been scavenged from the shoal area. Local people were quick to gather the timbers of these wrecked ships as they floated into shore for free and easy firewood to heat their homes. The following list chronicles many of the ships that were grounded or wrecked on Ford Shoals from the period 1834 through 1919.

Augustus Ford

SHIP CASUALTIES ON FORD SHOALS

Ship	Date	Description
Oswego	5/13/1834	Schooner - stranded in a gale - got off
Jon P. Hale	10/30/1856	Scow-schooner - stranded in terrible snow storm - some cargo, rigging, sails, and spars removed - ship may have been recovered
Victoria	10/9/1871	Schooner - went to pieces
Peerless	11/26/1872	Schooner
Meteor	4/12/1874	Schooner - ice laden and under tow sank on shoal
S. D. Gilson	8/2/1874	Steam canal boat - stranded - pulled off by tug

David W. Mills. Image courtesy of the Great Lakes Historical Society Collection of the Historical Collection of the Great Lakes at Bowling Green State University

Kate Kelly	11/1/1874	Schooner - grounded
Speedwell	11/13/1878	Schooner - lightered then pulled off by tug
Dominion	11/20/1879	Schooner - badly strained and broken - stripped of rigging - went to pieces
Carrie & Cora	11/9/1882	Canal boat - foundered while being towed - went to pieces on shoal
George Finney	11/1/1883	Schooner - stranded in a snowstorm - recovered three weeks later
Agnes Hope	11/7/1884	Schooner - stranded and broke up
Belle Wilson	11/15/1886	Steamer - broke rudder and drifted around lake in snowstorm - grounded on shoal - may have been pulled off
Julia	12/8/1887	Schooner - stranded on shoal in blinding snowstorm - may have been released by Donnelly Wrecking Company
D. Freeman	8/13/1888	Schooner - went on shoal in heavy summer storm - may be total loss
St. Joseph	6/27/1903	Steamer - stranded in fog - pulled off
Dauntless	4/28/1908	Tug - towing barges, tipped over and wrecked - pieces coming off
David W. Mill	8/11/1919	Steamer - stranded in dense fog - total wreck - many pieces came to shore - ribs of wreck remain today

MEXICO BAY: GRAVEYARD OF SHIPS

The Graveyard of Lake Ontario is the sinister name given to the eastern end of the lake called Mexico Bay. The Bay area extends from the Oswego, New York harbor 40 miles northeast to Stoney Point near Henderson Harbor at the eastern end of the lakeshore. The prevailing winds on Lake Ontario are from the west and northwest. Sailing ships in peril from severe storms would run with the winds to save themselves. This was a common maneuver that captains sailing in the open seas would use to save their ship. On Lake Ontario, running with a west or northwest wind would bring a ship into the area of Mexico Bay and beyond all hope of safety. Once driven into the bay by a gale, it was nearly impossible for a sailing ship to work its way out; inevitably, they would be driven ashore or into the shallow areas 200-300 yards from shore. At this distance from shore, most crews did not survive the shipwreck. From 1840 through 1877, Port Ontario was the only harbor of refuge in Mexico Bay. Maintaining this harbor was difficult and expensive, as lake currents at this end of the lake move large quantities of sand around, which requires constant dredging in order to allow ships to pass safely into the harbor.

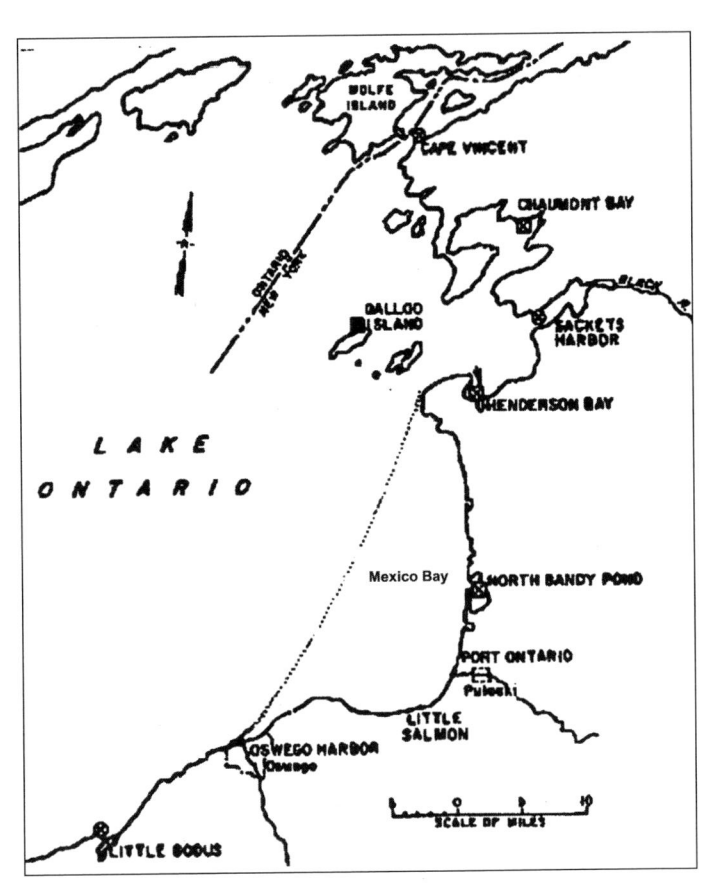

Map of Mexico Bay and Eastern Lake Ontario.
Image courtesy of Jim Kennard

In 1877, Port Ontario ceased to be a port of entry as commerce and trade moved elsewhere. In 1874, the Big Sandy Life Saving Station was established in Mexico Bay at the mouth of Big Sandy Creek near Port Ontario to aid sailing vessels stranded or wrecked in this area of Lake Ontario. By the 1920s, sailing ships on Lake Ontario had all but disappeared and there was no longer a need for a lifesaving station in Mexico Bay. Lifesaving operations were moved to a station on Gallop Island. The Big Sandy station continued to be supported into the 1930s, but it was mainly used to handle small boats in distress. One would think that Mexico Bay would be a shipwreck hunters paradise, however this is not so. Today, there are only a few scarce remains of ships that wrecked here. Most of the ships wrecked near or on shore, were pounded to pieces in the weeks that followed. Winter ice ground up what was left of a ship and the large movement of sand covered up whatever pieces remained.

Shipwreck in Mexico Bay.   Watercolor by Roland E. Stevens III

Mexico Bay: Graveyard of Ships

Some of the ships that have wrecked in Mexico Bay in the 1800s:

Coopers Floating Battery — 7-6-1813 — Built to protect Sackets Harbor
Floating Fortress — "stove to pieces" breaking up with wreckage coming ashore.

Fair American — 10-1818 — Wrecked off mouth of Salmon River.
Schooner

Asp — 10-11-1820 — Capsized, then drifted across the lake and finally went ashore on the bar at Salmon River and broke up quickly.
Schooner

Atlas — 12-13-1822 — Wrecked near Salmon River.
Schooner

Medora — 11-11-1835 — Went ashore near the mouth of Big Sandy Creek laden with wheat and walnuts, all hands lost. The bodies of a man and woman were taken from the cabin.
Schooner

John Marshall — 10-18-1844 — Wrecked ashore near Stoney Point - broken into pieces.
Schooner

Halifax — 12-5-1854 — Anchored off Little Sandy Creek, New York, to ride out a gale. After two days, her anchors slipped and she went ashore and became a total wreck two miles below Port Ontario.
Schooner

J. B. Collins — 11-16-1855 — Sprang a leak, tried to make it to Port Ontario. She went ashore nearby and broke in two.
Schooner

Pigeon — 9-1-1859 — Bound from Port Ontario to Genesee. Went ashore three miles south of Big Sandy Creek.
Schooner

Sodus — 9-1-1859 — Bound from Port Ontario to Genesee. Went ashore about three miles north of Big Sandy Creek.
Schooner

J.S. Harvey — 12-8-1865 — Became unmanageable and went ashore at dusk. Part of her cargo was salvaged, but the ship was a total loss near Little Salmon River.
Brigantine

Laurel — 8-22-1876 — Foundered in a storm 1½ miles off Big Sandy Creek in seven fathoms of water. May have been removed.
Schooner

Utica Sidewheel Steamer	4-17-1850	Her skipper mistook the lights at Port Ontario for those at Oswego and tried to put in, striking the pier and going ashore near Port Ontario - never recovered.
Cortez Schooner	11-12-1880	Driven ashore in a storm - 3 miles north of Big Sandy lifesaving station. Cargo of wheat partially salvaged - ship went to pieces.
Ariadne Schooner	11-30-1886	Driven ashore by a gale, she went to pieces a few miles east of Sandy Creek Life Saving Station near Big Sandy Creek.
John Burt Schooner	9-26-1892	Wrecked near the mouth of Big Sandy Creek - a portion of the wreck is still visible during low lake levels.
Hartford Schooner	10-11-1894	Foundered in 40 feet of water near the mouth of the Little Sandy Pond - later broken up by waves, ice, and the swelling of her cargo - small section of the wreck exists today.

SUNKEN HOUSEBOATS OFF OSWEGO

While searching for historic shipwrecks off Oswego, we occasionally find modern boats on the bottom of Lake Ontario, the majority of which have been houseboats. Experienced boaters know that the lake can sometimes change very rapidly from calm waters into high waves without much warning. Taking a houseboat on a 50- mile journey across the lake from Oswego to Kingston or the St. Lawrence River can be a perilous journey with a very high potential of risk. Houseboats are not designed to accommodate large waves more than a few feet. Over the years, some people who took that risk lost their boat and often their lives.

Here are a few of the houseboats that sank off Oswego:

CHUG-A-LUG

With a final "*Glug, Glug, Glug,*" this yet-to-be-identified houseboat ended in 337 feet of water about 6 miles north of Oswego. The heavy growth of mussels on the boat would indicate it has been on the bottom for a long time. A New York registration number of *NY 1921 DS* appears above one of the side windows. Perhaps someone can remember the details of this long gone houseboat.

Houseboat *Chug-A-Lug*.
Image courtesy of Roger Pawlowski

SEA ROVER

In September 1973, the owner of a shipyard in Clayton, New York, set out on Lake Ontario to deliver a 32-foot houseboat to its new owner in Oswego. He was last seen around 6 p.m. at a marina in Cape Vincent where he filled both gas tanks for the 50+ mile trip to Oswego. Travelling at night added another level of risk to his lake journey. The houseboat sank in deep water en route between Galloo Island light and Oswego. His body was never found.

E ZEE CRUZ'N

In July 2003, grandparents with a three-year-old child, attempting to return to Canada, encountered six-foot waves which overturned their houseboat eight miles off Oswego. They had been advised by the US Coast Guard not to set out in the lake, but decided to go anyway. They radioed the Coast Guard for assistance but provided incorrect GPS coordinates. Fortunately, this happened during the 2003 Pro-Am Fishing Tournament and fishing boats *Trout One* and *Candy* saw the flares that were fired signaling distress. The *E Zee CRUZ'N* sank within a few minutes. The couple and young child were rescued by the fishermen and brought to the Oswego Coast Guard station for observation and then released.

HARBORFEST HOUSEBOAT

For a description of our fourth houseboat discovery, please see the next chapter "Recreational Diving on Shipwrecks Near Oswego."

Recreational Diving on Shipwrecks near Oswego

David W. Mills

The *David W. Mills* was an old wooden steamer 202-feet in length, built in 1874. On August 11, 1919, the steamship ran up on Ford Shoal four and a half miles west of Oswego. She was the victim of a bizarre set of circumstances. The smoke from a number of forest fires in Canada combined with summer humidity had blanketed Lake Ontario in a fog so thick that visual navigation was nearly impossible. The steamship departed Oswego at 5:30 a.m. Captain Matt Lanagan ordered the wheelman to steer the ship southwest with the hope of keeping the shoreline insight on the trip to Sodus. Before they could see land, the *David W. Mills* grounded several hundred feet onto Ford Shoal. Over the next few weeks the owners of the *Mills* conferred with the Donnelly Wrecking Company of Kingston, Ontario about removing the steamer from the shoal. Before any salvage operation could begin, storms and heavy seas began to tear the ship apart. A large portion of the bow broke off and came into shore along with pieces of timber which locals carted away for their own use. Eventually the *Mills* was stripped of her gear, life boats, and lighting fixtures. The steamer *David W. Mills* was the largest ship to have wrecked on Ford Shoals.

Side-scan sonar image of the *David W. Mills*.
Image courtesy of Jim Kennard

The wreck of the *David W. Mills* is Oswego's most popular recreational dive site. The steamer lies in 12 to 25 feet of water. The remains of the steamers' oak timbers are laid out over the bottom of the shoal area. A diver can swim the entire 180-foot length of the keel and along the propeller shaft. An 11-foot propeller with four massive blades is still attached to the end of the shaft. Off to the port side of the wreck is an engine boiler which lies only a foot below the surface of the lake. The winch can be found toward the bow with chain still wrapped around it. The chain leads off to the ship's anchor 100 feet in the distance.

Four easily dived wrecks near Oswego.

The Oswego Maritime Foundation has created a guide to the *David W. Mills* shipwreck. It's available by contacting the H. Lee White Maritime Museum at 315-342-0480, or by stopping at the museum office located at 1 West First Street in Oswego, New York.

Location: N 43° 26.630' W 76° 35.089'

SOURCES:

Oswego Palladium, August 11, 1919.
_____, August 12, 1919.
_____, August 14, 1919.
_____, August 15, 1919.
_____, August 18, 1919.
_____, August 22, 1919.
_____, August 27, 1919.
_____, August 30, 1919.
_____, September 11, 1919.
_____, September 16, 1919.
_____, September 17, 1919.
_____, September 19, 1919.
_____, October 7, 1919.
Oswego Daily Times, October 7, 1919.

TUG *CORMORANT*

The tug *Cormorant* was within a few miles of Oswego on its return from work on the St. Lawrence Seaway on October 16, 1958 when it encountered a fierce thunderstorm. High waves washed on board the tug flooding the engine room. Without power the pumps were unable to expel the water which soon swamped the *Cormorant*. The tug sank in 120 feet of water 3.3 miles northeast of Oswego. The men on board escaped by using the inner tube from a tractor and a raft of boards which they had picked out of the St. Lawrence River. The crew drifted on the lake for nearly 20 hours. The following day, as they got closer to shore, a local hunter saw them and followed the raft along until he was able walk out into the lake and help the men to dry land. The depth of the water has protected the tug from the destruction of heavy wave action and ice. This is the only recreational dive (under 135 feet) of a shipwreck near Oswego in which the entire vessel is still intact. Most of the time visibility is clear enough for a diver to see the entire 43-foot length of the tug. Shipwreck searchers Tim Shippee, Doug Low, Dennis Gerber, and Captain Peter Tombolillo located the *Cormorant* in the summer of 1996.

Tug *Cormorant* underwater. Image courtesy of Roger Pawlowski

Location: N 43° 30.787' W 76° 30.290'

SOURCES:

Oswego Palladium-Times, October 17, 1958.
_____, October 18, 1958.

TUGBOAT *MARY KAY*

Two miles west of Oswego harbor lies the battered remains of the tug *Mary Kay*. On September 21, 1988, the *Mary Kay* left Rochester, New York for the port of Boston. As the tug was approaching Oswego high winds on the lake created two 9 foot waves that crashed over her stern swamping the engine room. The *Mary Kay* listed and then quickly sank beneath the waves of Lake Ontario. The two-man crew radioed the Coast Guard for help just before the tug capsized and they were thrown overboard. The men were in the water for nearly 30 minutes until the rubber raft on the tug automatically inflated and rose to the surface. They crawled into the raft and waited a short time before the rescuers from the Oswego Coast Guard station arrived to pick them up. The *Mary Kay* was built in 1957 as a 55-foot, 35-ton tugboat powered by twin Murphy diesel engines. The Salvage and Demolition Company of North Weymouth, Massachusetts purchased the tug in 1988 and re-fitted her prior to the journey to Boston. Wave action and ice packs have been wearing down the tug's remains for 30 years. The stern and mid-ships that once stood tall on the rocky bottom have now crumbled in the shallow depth of 41 feet where she lies. Divers can still see the two propellers, bollard posts, and the twin diesel engines. Schools of bass can be seen in and around the shipwreck.

Location: N 43° 27.705' W 76° 33.198'

SOURCES:

Post Standard [Syracuse, New York], September 22, 1988.
_____, September 23, 1988.
_____, September 29, 1988.
Oswego Palladium-Times, September 26, 1988.
_____, October 24, 1988.
_____, October 26, 1988.

"Harborfest Houseboat"

During Harborfest '93, northwest winds were kicking up eight-foot waves on Lake Ontario. A 32-foot houseboat was out on the lake that day. The little, calm-water vessel didn't stand a chance, and foundered in 32 feet of water two miles west of Oswego Harbor. The two men aboard were rescued by the Coast Guard. The houseboat is now the new home of plenty of bass and perch. The real name of the vessel is all but forgotten. Local divers began referring to it as the "Harborfest Houseboat." The name stuck after it appeared in a newspaper's trivia article in 1996.

Location: N 43° 27.470' W 76° 33.335'

Authors' Biographies

Jim Kennard has been diving and exploring the lakes of the northeast United States since 1970. He's found more than 200 shipwrecks in the Great Lakes, Lake Champlain, the New York Finger Lakes, and in the Mississippi and Ohio Rivers. Utilizing his background as an electrical engineer, he built a side-scan sonar system that located many of these shipwrecks. Significant discoveries include the two oldest shipwrecks discovered in the Great Lakes, the 1780 British warship HMS *Ontario* and the sloop *Washington* lost in 1803. In 1983 he found a unique horse powered ferryboat in Lake Champlain. All of these discoveries received worldwide attention in the news media. Discoveries made by Jim and his shipwreck teams have appeared in a number of publications including *National Geographic, Sea Technology, Inland Seas, Wreck Diving, Skin Diver,* and several Rochester, New York publications. He's appeared on Discovery Channel, CBC, BBC, and FOX News.

In 2013 he was selected a Fellow of The Explorers Club. Jim received the Joyce S. Hayward Award for Historic Interpretation from the Association for Great Lakes Maritime History in 2015 for documenting the stories of Great Lakes shipwreck discoveries on his website www.shipwreckworld.com.

Jim graduated from Clarkson University with a Bachelor of Science in electrical engineering in 1966. In addition to searching for elusive shipwrecks Jim has been an amateur radio operator since he was 13 and starting hiking at 65. He's climbed over 100 peaks in the Catskill Mountains and all of the 46 high peaks in the Adirondacks. A native of Peekskill he lives in Fairport, New York with his wife Marilyn.

Born and raised in Buffalo, **Roger Pawlowski** graduated from The State University of New York at Buffalo in 1972 with Bachelors and Masters degrees in electrical engineering. He served in the Air Force as an active duty pilot and then in the Reserves flying C-130 aircraft for 25 years. In 1990 he deployed to Iraq to serve in Desert Storm. Roger retired from the Air Force Reserves as a Lt. Col. in 1996.

He and his wife Patricia raised three sons in Rochester, New York and now enjoy time with their four grandchildren. Roger worked for Harris Corporation for 27 years until he left to purchase and grow an electrical product design and manufacturing business with two partners. Seven years later they sold the business after growing revenues. Roger retired from Ultralife Batteries Corporation after five years and now runs his own engineering consulting business.

Jim Kennard and Roger knew each other from their time together at Harris Corporation. In 1980, while flying a practice mission over Lake Ontario, Roger witnessed a small aircraft plunge into the lake. His details of the incident and location helped Jim locate the aircraft which had crashed several miles from shore and in a depth of over 100 feet.

Semi-retirement gave Roger the time to pursue new adventures and scuba diving on shipwrecks in the northeast and Pacific Ocean gave him a focus. Roger joined the shipwreck discovery team in 2011. He's the owner/operator of the search boat and the remote operated vehicle that provides the video imaging of the shipwrecks located by the side-scan sonar. He also designs some of the equipment needed for deep water exploration.

Born in Chicago in 1940, **Roland "Chip" Stevens** grew up in Rochester and Pultneyville, New York. He graduated with a Bachelor of Science degree from the University of Rochester and earned a Bachelor of Architecture and a Master of Architecture in urban design from Syracuse University in 1973. For forty-five years he worked as a County Planner and New York State Registered Architect. Upon graduation from Syracuse, Roland studied privately with Jossey Bilan, a noted painter in Keene, New York. In addition to painting, which he has been pursuing more avidly since retiring, he's found more time to sail, ski, travel, and search for shipwrecks.

Roland Stevens resides in Pultneyville, New York with his wife Georgia, his enthusiastic supporter. For over 70 years he has been a downhill and cross country skier. Roland even tried ski jumping for several years and was on the National Ski Patrol for 15 years. Other interests include Scottish bagpiping in several pipe bands for more than 30 years, amateur archaeologist for 60 years, shipwreck explorer and team artist for the last 14 years.